C000258978

EAT BIKE COOK

First published in the UK in 2021 by

Kitchen Press Ltd
1 Windsor Place
Dundee
DD2 1BG

Photography by Alan Donaldson
Design by Andrew Forteath

ISBN 978-1-9163165-4-6

1 2 3 4 5 6 7 8 9 10

A catalogue record for this book is available from the British Library

Printed in India

EAT BIKE COOK

KITTY PEMBERTON-PLATT
AND FI BUCHANAN

KITCHEN PRESS

CONTENTS

RECIPES

It was the winter of 2015 when I first started what could be considered a real training programme for cycling. After diving headfirst and blindfolded into the world of bike racing at the beginning of that year, by the end, I had decided I had what it took and my next goal was to make the team for the Olympics. It seemed not just lofty as ambitions go but really rather ridiculous, but I've always been an all-or-nothing type of person and that clearly applied to my cycling too. I had no idea what I'd let myself in for – how hard it would be, how much I had to learn and how much I would need to eat.

FOREWORD BY

LIZZY BANKS

That winter I can honestly say I've never been so hungry in my life. My body suddenly faced the huge shock that came with going from nearly zero to a semi-full-time training programme. I had never trained for anything in my life before, and I simply couldn't keep up with the calorie intake required. I did what any sensible 25-year-old in my position would do and devoured box after box of McVitie's Jaffa Cakes. The chocolatey-orange cakey delight wasn't my only fuelling strategy though: Party Rings, bourbon biscuits and heaps of pasta made the cut too.

After propping up the British biscuit industry for a good few months, I realised that in all likelihood this was, unfortunately, probably not the fuel of champions. As my body began to adjust to the effort required for training, I began to understand how to fuel my body better and, importantly, when to fuel my body. 'Fuel for the work required' is my training mantra these days, and if you're not sure if you've fuelled quite enough, then chuck in a bit extra for good measure. The risk of under-fuelling is far greater than the risk of over-fuelling.

What I've learnt is that it's okay to not like porridge (I hate it and much prefer a bowl of Crunchy Nut Cornflakes or a few double toasted crumpets in the morning), and despite what Instagram tells you, successful athletes do not just eat salad for dinner. As with anything, life is all about balance. Think about how many calories you are spending whilst exercising, then think about how many you are consuming during the exercise. Do you have a good balance there? A huge deficit during exercise is only going to make you far hungrier (and if you're anything like me, far grumpier too) later on. Love your body, give it what it needs. And if it says that sometimes what it needs is cake, then, you know what? Eat some cake.

Lizzy Banks.

My road cycling journey began when I bought a second-hand bike at the age of 24. I mistakenly wore shorts over bib tights and regularly fell out of my clipped-in pedals at traffic lights, but I was enchanted. The bike, and its surrounding culture, quickly became the lens through which I navigated my day-to-day life, as I found myself moving from a novice to club rider to amateur racer. All the adventures I had and lessons I learned on the bike supported my personal growth off the bike.

INTRODUCTION BY

KITTY PEMBERTON -PLATT

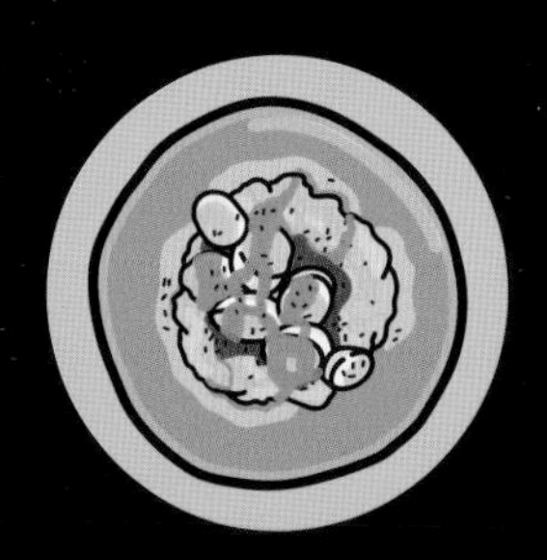

While the health and fitness benefits were rewarding, it was the relationships, conversations and experiences that were truly addictive. Sharing moments of heightened emotion and vulnerability with others kept me consistently returning to this community.

One of those experiences was the joy of eating and talking about food with other cyclists – from perfecting my morning oats recipe and researching new cafés, to developing a pre-race routine and finish-line reward. The food we enjoy around the bike is much more than fuel; it's raw and honest human connection, baked-in effort followed by fulfilment. Communal meals and good conversation after a ride – whether on a petrol station forecourt or in a café – can instantly silence our internal chatter and steady our minds to focus on the present.

This charming culinary world led me to design the first Food for Sport illustrations. It started as a small project I shared on social media, visualising the menu choices of female cyclists. People seemed to connect with the honesty and simplicity of the diaries and responded to seeing the food we enjoy around the bike illustrated in such detail.

When I received a message from a female cyclist saying 'I now feel so much better about eating on the bike, and will allow myself to fuel properly,' I realised that even though they appeared light-hearted, these illustrated food diaries could be a valuable way of offering guidance and support with our often complicated relationship with food.

Eat Bike Cook features nineteen stories from the saddle, rides remembered through the food that fuelled them. Fi Buchanan took her inspiration from these food stories and created recipes that can be enjoyed at every stage of your ride. Dotted throughout, you'll also find snackable advice born from emotional and nutritional lessons on the bike.

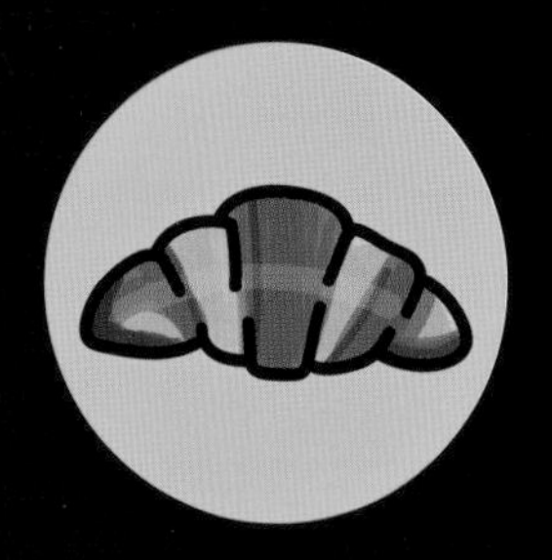

The book is a playful celebration of the food we enjoy around cycling – an insight into the preferences, rituals and tastes of women around the world. It champions a positive attitude and holistic kindness to our minds and bodies.

I'm so passionate about showing how women's sport and its surrounding culture can create a rewarding and desirable way of life. Thank you to all the women who have supported me and shared their rides, stories and, quite often, back pocket food with me. I truly hope this book encourages more moments of joy and connection and you find yourself surrounded by good people, beautifully baked pastries and perfectly poured coffee. Or a pot of soup and a Hobnob, if that's your thing.

See you at a café soon (black filter and an almond croissant, please).

Kitty
@kittypp
@_apressport

The food diaries in this book illustrate the diverse diets of cyclists, from foraged berries and greens and mindful overnight oats, to joyous pizza and beer or steak and red wine. The food choices cyclists make are about something larger than the exchange of effort for fuel. They are about the freedom to make your own choices and about listening to your body, health and happiness.

Eat Bike Cook isn't about sports nutrition – it won't give you the optimal diet for peak athletic performance. What it will give you is an insight into what women cyclists eat and why their food choices work for them. Because what you eat – or, in other words, how you choose to fuel, maintain and ultimately rebuild your body – does matter. With an understanding of the basics of nutrition you can give your body what it needs, when it needs it.

THE BASICS

Sometimes that might be a carbonara and a salad, and other times it may be a Mars bar and a handful of Haribo. It's not just balancing what you burn with what you consume; it's striking a balance between sustaining, nutritious foods and short-term, energy-boosting ones.

You need to fuel your body for activity and to do this effectively, you need an understanding of how your body processes food and converts it into energy.

CARBS ARE KING

When it comes to energy and fuel for sport, carbs are number one. They're the primary energy source for your body, and before, during and after you do a hard workout, your body needs them for fuel.

All carbohydrates break down into sugars, or glucose, in the body and provide fuel for the brain and muscles during activity. If the carbohydrates don't get used, the body stores them as fat. There are two types of carbohydrate: simple and complex. Simple carbohydrates produce fast-access, or short-chain, sugars. They're made up of shorter chains of sugar molecules and the body breaks them down more easily, giving a short-term energy boost. They are found in sugary drinks and foods such as cake, chocolate, fruit and honey, as well as energy gels and bars.

Complex carbohydrates are made of longer chains of sugar molecules and take the body more time to break down, and so provide a more long-term sustaining energy. They are higher in fibre and nutrients and so digest more slowly. Wholegrain bread, pasta, potatoes and rice are all complex carbohydrates. Complex carbohydrates are broken down and stored in the muscles and liver as glycogen. During exercise, when your body needs more energy, the glycogen is converted back into glucose and used for fuel.

NO BONKING!

When you have burned through the available energy that your body has stored, you can experience what's known as 'bonking' – weakness and extreme fatigue when you have depleted all of your reserves and simply can't cycle any further. Runners call it 'hitting the wall', and you will know when it has happened to you because that's how it feels. See page 61 for tips on how to avoid bonking.

PROTEIN

This is the nutrient that builds and repairs your organs, muscles and skin and provides your body with the amino acids it needs to produce hormones. Research has shown that people who enjoy regular athletic and sporting activity have an increased need for tissue repair, so making sure that you are including enough protein in your diet is vital. Good sources of protein are fish, lean meat, beans and pulses, nuts, eggs and low-fat dairy products.

Although traditionally the Western diet concentrates most of its protein intake in the last meal of the day, your body can't store protein so a better balance can be achieved if you spread your intake throughout the day.

FATS

While there are healthy and less healthy versions of this group, fats are a critical part of a balanced diet, so don't be tempted to exclude them from your diet because of scaremongering from a less enlightened age.

The fats found in plants, nuts, seeds and fish are beneficial and your body thrives on them. They enhance cell, nerve and brain health, and ensure that your body can process the fat-soluble vitamins A, D, E and K. A good example of this is enjoying kale, which is full of vitamin K, with an olive oil-based dressing. Good fats/oils can be found in avocados, olive oil, nut butters, coconut oil, mixed nuts, whole eggs, oily fish like salmon, and cheese in moderation.

Don't overdo hydrogenated fats and saturated fats in your daily diet. They are the fats that will clog your arteries and increase your cholesterol. You'll find them in chips, biscuits, donuts, cakes and processed snack foods like microwave popcorn.

VITAMINS AND MINERALS

The best way to take on vitamins and minerals is to eat a diverse and colourful diet. Aim for at least five pieces of fruit and vegetables a day and, as twee as it sounds, 'eat a rainbow' as the vitamins and minerals you need tend to be found in intensely coloured vegetables such as kale, broccoli, purple cabbage, tomatoes, peppers and pomegranates.

Vitamins A, D, E and K need to be ingested with fat in order to be efficiently absorbed by the body. Vitamin A strengthens the immune system and helps keep skin healthy, vitamin D helps keep bones, teeth and muscles healthy, vitamin E strengthens the immune system and maintains healthy eyes and vitamin K helps healing and blood clotting.

There are certain vitamins and minerals that are particularly important to the wellbeing of active women. The vitamin B group aids the metabolism and lifts energy levels. Calcium has been shown to help in stabilising blood pressure as well as maintaining bone health and brain function. Iron produces the red blood cells that carry oxygen around the body. Zinc is really important for immune function, metabolism and growth. And some research has suggested that magnesium, as a supplement, may be helpful if you are prone to muscle cramps.

HYDRATION

The human body is made up of at least 60 percent water and you need it to function healthily: we can survive for weeks without food but only a few days without water. It is essential for flushing toxins and waste from the body in the form of urine and for maintaining healthy digestive function. It regulates body temperature through sweating, it lubricates the joints and it helps to transport oxygen around the body in blood. It is crucial to maintain healthy hydration levels, especially when exercising as we lose a lot of water through sweat.

Take a long-term view on this and keep up with day-to-day hydration – make sure you're hitting the recommended daily amount of 2 litres of water per day. It's easy to monitor this by regularly checking your pee and ensuring it remains pale in colour. In the same way as you can bonk from insufficient energy supplies, you can bonk from dehydration.

LISTEN TO YOUR BODY

The food diaries show us how women cyclists at all levels, from weekend circuit cyclists to long-distance endurance riders and professional racers, engage with nutrition and use it in the practice of their sport. What we learn from the diaries is that there is no fixed prescription or perfect diet – only what works for you. Feel your energy, and adjust when you need to. Eat for your strongest self. Eat what's right for you.

BARBORA SOJKOVA

AGE 28
OXFORD, UK

ROAD RIDER

THE RIDE

A summer solo-ride across Europe to transport my bike from Prague (where I am from) to Oxford. I cycled 120km a day.

I decided to bikepack the 1247km from Prague to Oxford, despite having no experience of long-distance solo bike travel. I packed my tarp and sleeping bag and cycled on average 120km a day across the Continent to Hoek van Holland to catch the ferry over to East Anglia. I slept in forests, sheds, little German stone towers, and even spent a night in the famous Bauhaus architecture school, where you can rent a room and it is absolutely amazing. There were many highs and lows along the way, as you can imagine. Cycling brings such a constant flux of emotions; if you add the solitude to it, you get a very strange cocktail. I battled that strange place with food, of course.

It was July, so I constantly picked berries from beside the road. I stopped in cute German villages at farmers' markets. I bought flat peaches in every single supermarket along the way, and the German institution of the *Bäckerei & Konditorei* (bakery and pastry shop) became the true saviour of the trip and of my sanity.

Who does not love a massive slab of traditional continental cherry pie, right? My point being, if I am at home and training properly, I think a lot about what I eat but when I became a really vulnerable human being on the road – 'a little sack of emotions' – as we would say in Czech, I ate guided purely by how I felt. It was one of the best decisions ever.

BAUHAUS
PRAGUE TO OXFORD
EAST ANGLIA
"a little sack of emotions"
Ferry
OXFORD
PRAGUE
Deutsche Markt
Beeren
Kirschkuchen
Brezel
Crepes

PRE-

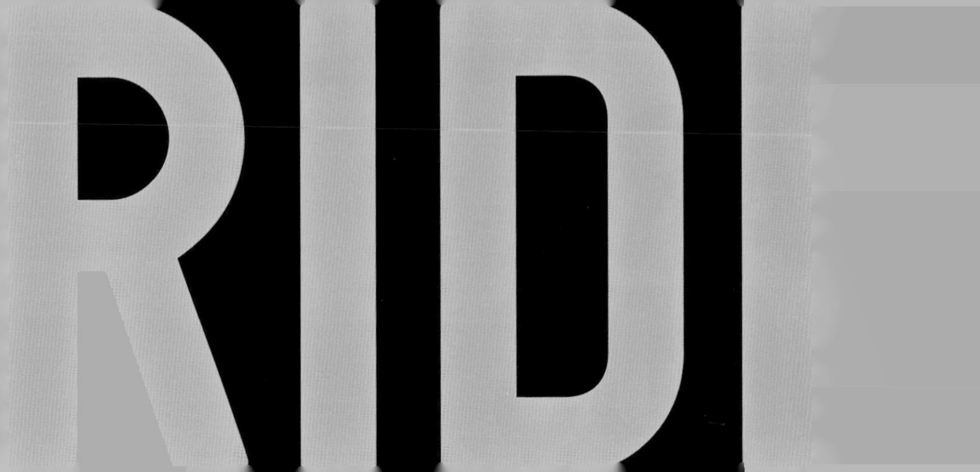
RID

The best head start you can give yourself in preparation for a cycle is to enjoy a generally healthy daily diet, keep well hydrated and eat a nutritionally balanced meal the evening before your ride. And then there's breakfast – you absolutely shouldn't skip it. Make time to prepare the food you enjoy. Allow a couple of hours if you prefer a substantial breakfast and less for a smaller meal. There's a lot to be said for allowing time for ritual and a period of calm. An early bird might prepare Power Oats (p.32) with peanut butter and honey, while a late riser might have a square of Blueberry and Walnut Baked Oats (p.51) and a coffee before setting off.

PRE-RIDE STAR FOODS

OATS

Affordable, customisable and highly nutritious, oats might well be the ultimate sports food. All oats (even instant) are wholegrains and are high in fibre and plant-based protein. They are complex carbohydrates so provide a more consistent source of energy. They contain vitamins A, B1, B2 and B6 as well as the minerals magnesium and zinc. Because of their high fibre content, they retain water and help to keep your body hydrated. Choose honey, fresh fruit or spices to sweeten them instead of processed white sugar.

EGGS

Pocket-sized, delicious, nutritious and packaged in their own environmentally friendly little cases, eggs are the adventurer's best friend. Whilst much is made of the protein-rich egg white, the whole egg is your superfood. The yolk has cholesterol, true, but also a complex blend of vitamins, minerals and protein, including choline, which is used by endurance athletes to delay fatigue. Each egg is a natural package of protein, B vitamins, magnesium and zinc. When possible, choose organic eggs as the hens are not fed GM corn and there is no routine use of antibiotics.

COFFEE

Studies have shown that there are real advantages to enjoying a coffee before you cycle as a pre-sport performance enhancer. A study published in the British Journal of Sport Medicine concluded that drinking coffee significantly improved performance of sustained high-intensity exercise. The caffeine in coffee increases epinephrine (adrenal) levels in the blood. This is the 'fight or flight' hormone, preparing you for intense physical exertion, and separate research has shown that this increase can improve sprint performance, increase cycling endurance and reduce your perception of muscle pain. However, beware – too much can have extremely uncomfortable side effects, including insomnia, muscle tremors, irritability and headaches. The recommended daily amount is up to 400mg, the equivalent of up to four cups of coffee.

JO SPENCER

AGE 36
WILTSHIRE, UK

ROAD AND OFF-ROAD RIDER

Enjoys solo road rides for thinking time on her day off (she is an NHS doctor), 10-mile time trials, off-road rides on her cross-country bike and, during the week and in colder months, watt-biking using Zwift.

THE RIDE

An 82km group-training ride with the Wheelers Cycle Club, with a 5.5km warm up and 10km cool down.

PRE-RIDE

The day started with a bowl of **tropical granola** with coconut milk (extra tropical) and a double espresso from Carlos – our long-serving and faithful bean-to-cup machine.

DURING

I took two bidons with electrolytes and four Torq gels in a range of flavours (my favourite is banoffee), as well as a 20g cookies-and-cream flavoured OTE Duo Bar (they're like Rice Krispie bars – delicious and very easy to eat on or off the bike).

After the warm up I ate one of the Duo Bars, then at the café stop I had a cinnamon bun and a flat white with oat milk.

Between us, we put the world to rights before setting off on the journey home.

POST-RIDE

Before my shower I had a cookies-and-cream recovery protein shake with almond milk. Lunch was pitta pizzas – two wholemeal pitta breads with tomato paste, halved cherry tomatoes, oregano and mozzarella – followed by a packet of sweet chilli Sun Bites crisps. Then it was feet-up time: a snuggly blanket and a sofa snooze!

ADVICE

- Don't wait until you're hungry to eat – once the bonk hits it's difficult to come back from it. Fuel up every 30–40 minutes with a gel or solid snack and always take a bit more than you think you'll eat in your back pocket. You never know when you (or a pal) might need it.
- Be careful when eating gels – no one wants sticky gel on their handlebars for the rest of their ride!

TROPICAL GRANOLA, P.24

TROPICAL GRANOLA
double shot please
PITTA PIZZAS
start
THE RIDE
82KM TRAINING RIDE
end
pre shower
Fave!
COOKIES +CREAM
THE STOP
Famous
&
=
good conversation

TROPICAL GRANOLA

MAKES 12 SERVINGS

250g rolled or jumbo oats (not instant)

100g coconut flakes

75g ground almonds

100g raw cashews

30g ground flax seed

75ml runny honey

70ml olive oil or melted coconut oil

70ml maple syrup

2 tsp vanilla extract

¼ tsp sea salt

100g dried mango, chopped

100g dried pineapple, chopped

Shop-bought granola just doesn't compare to this deliciously moreish homemade version. Feel free to customise with what you have and what you like.

Preheat your oven to 180°C/160°C fan and line a large baking tray with greaseproof paper.

Place all the ingredients, except the mango and pineapple, in a large bowl and stir well. Then spread onto the baking tray in an even layer.

Bake on the middle shelf of your oven for 25–30 minutes. Every 10 minutes take out the tray and, using a wooden spatula, give everything a shuffle to make sure it's all toasting evenly.

When the granola is golden, remove it from the oven, add the dried fruit and mix well.

Allow to cool thoroughly before transferring to a big jar or airtight container. It will keep for 2 weeks.

Roasted fresh coconut
Use a vegetable peeler to cut thin strips of coconut straight out of the shell. Roast at 170°C/150°C fan for 5–10 minutes, checking often to ensure they don't burn. For a sweet treat, toss the strips in maple syrup before roasting.

LARA KAZAKOS

AGE 31
LUCERNE, SWITZLERAND

ROAD RIDER

Enjoys long rides in the mountains as well as short, fast racing.

THE RIDE

L'Étape du Tour – 180km. This is an amateur cycling event on a Tour de France stage.

PRE-RIDE

At 5am I had oats prepared the night before (oats, milk, banana, honey and a sachet of vanilla protein powder) in a McDonald's cup (I forgot a container!). Immediately before setting off at 6.30am I had a banana.

DURING

- Three mini brioches with ham, avocado and cheese wrapped in tin foil, not plastic.
- Four Clif bars (mixed flavours, but oatmeal raisin or coconut chocolate chip FTW).
- Two pre-packaged chocolate crêpes (melted to perfection by the first climb).
- Two caffeine gels (just before the BIG climbs).
- Half a banana and an emergency cup of Coke (last feed-stop!).
- Ten bidons of water (five with electrolyte tabs) – the temperature on the ride peaked at 35 degrees!

POST-RIDE

Cheese and bacon burger and frites. A gin and tonic – and more water!

ADVICE

- Wrap sandwiches in tin foil instead of plastic; otherwise they get squashed and are impossible to get into while riding. Tin foil is also recyclable.

FRITE FINISH

à votre santé

BIRCHER MUESLI WITH RASPBERRY COMPOTE

SERVES 1

for the bircher

30g rolled or jumbo oats

1 apple, skin on, grated

30g dried cranberries

30g pecans or hazelnuts, roughly chopped

10g seeds (such as pumpkin, sunflower, chia, sesame or flax)

juice of 1 medium orange, or the equivalent splash of your preferred milk

for the raspberry compote

150g raspberries, frozen or fresh

1 tbsp lemon juice

2 tbsp water

3 tbsp sugar

to serve

Greek yoghurt

Soaking the bircher for a couple of hours, or ideally overnight, makes it easier to digest and gives it a softer texture. This makes more compote than you need for one serving but it will last for several days in the fridge.

Mix all the ingredients for the bircher together in your serving bowl. Cover and refrigerate overnight so it's ready for the morning.

For the compote, add everything to a smallish pan and bring to a simmer over a low heat. Don't allow it to come to a boil. Simmer for 10 minutes or so, then strain, while still warm, through a fine sieve into a jar.

Enjoy your bircher with a tablespoon or two of cold, zingy Greek yoghurt and a colourful splash of raspberry compote for a thoroughly energising start to the day.

Add a pinch of cinnamon to the mix for comforting warmth on colder days, and replace the compote with handfuls of fresh strawberries and raspberries on warmer days.

KITTY PEMBERTON-PLATT

AGE 31
LONDON, UK

ROAD RIDER

Always looking for the next outdoor adventure that finishes with food, drink and good company.

THE RIDE

100km Essex Road Ride.

PRE-RIDE

I always get up early before a ride – I hate being rushed and I absolutely love everything about pre-sport breakfasts. My go-to is **oats** with sassy ingredients, which I soak overnight in oat milk then warm up the following morning. It sounds like a faff but once you've made it a few times it becomes second nature.

DURING

I have become an expert on back-pocket foods. On this ride I opted for two **blueberry and peanut butter wraps**. The shape fits perfectly in the centre of your jersey and the softer it becomes, the more satisfying it tastes. The snacks before and after the main event were a Squares Bar (after a tip off from Hannah Barnes) and a Veloforte bar – the chocolate one is divine.

POST-RIDE

I often down some water (and chocolate milk, if I've got it) as soon as I'm back, which keeps me going whilst I shower. I then make sure I have a proper meal after the marathon of snacking all day. My favourite is my take on a **Japanese omelette**. I'm usually peckish for the rest of the day and find Greek yoghurt with sweet additions like fruit, broken-up granola bars and honey is a good stopgap before dinner.

ADVICE

- Don't underestimate the importance of hydration.
- Keep your fuels topped up even if those around you aren't eating – all our bodies are different.
- You do end up eating a lot of sugar on a ride, so try to balance it out with savoury food when you get home.

POWER OATS, P.32; KITTY'S WRAP, P.68; KITTY'S OMURICE WITH CHEESE AND SPINACH, P.100

Veloforte
DATES + COCOA
THROW IT
ALL IN
CHOCO
MILK

POWER OATS

SERVES 1

50g rolled or jumbo oats

120ml oat milk

¼ tsp sea salt

1 medium, ripe banana, sliced

1 tbsp tahini

1 tbsp cacao nibs

1 tsp pumpkin or sesame seeds

1 tbsp honey

½ tsp cinnamon

This is Kitty's go-to oats recipe. The oats are soaked overnight then warmed gently in a saucepan which really does make a difference to the texture and flavour. Don't be tempted to microwave them. This recipe was inspired by one in Issy Croker's *Staying In, The Book*.

Place the oats, oat milk and sea salt in a small bowl and leave to soak overnight in the fridge.

When you're ready for breakfast, transfer the mixture to a small pan and heat over a medium heat. Stir occasionally until everything is warmed through and the mixture has started to thicken a little, about 2 minutes.

Transfer to a bowl and add the sliced banana, tahini, cacao nibs, pumpkin or sesame seeds, honey and cinnamon. Serve warm.

ALISON JACKSON

AGE 31
ALBERTA, CANADA

ROAD AND GRAVEL RIDER

Enjoys exploration rides, often with wandrer.earth – an app that uploads rides to Strava so you can see never-ridden roads and create new routes.

THE RIDE

140km Alberta prairie gravel endurance ride to find an old train trestle, plus a planned stop at a local coffee roaster.

PRE-RIDE

Coffee ritual: weigh my beans, hand-grind them, then bloom and brew in an Aeropress. Sip it black. I made **banana cinnamon pancakes** topped with almond butter and a heavy pour of Canadian maple syrup.

DURING

Oreo rice bars sliced and wrapped in squares (and sampled before leaving). Two stops to refill: one for a cortado (or two) and a soft cookie, and another stop for a Coke and water to finish the ride. Also, I always bring a protein bar for the last hour of the ride to start recovery early.

POST-RIDE

Recovery drink and a protein bar while I washed my bike then jumped in the shower before starting dinner prep.

Dinner was a sizzled rare bison **steak** from my family's bison ranch, with **chimichurri** sauce and **roasted sweet potatoes** and a glass of fine red wine. To finish, a couple of squares of sea salt dark chocolate went nicely with the last dregs of the vermilion pour.

ADVICE

- Wash your bike directly after the ride and before getting to the shower so the hard work is done, then you can focus fully on rest and relaxation.
- Long rides are more fun when there are more turns and changes of direction to keep you mentally engaged.
- Keep an eye on the wind direction: always start in a headwind so you can ride the tailwind home when you are more fatigued.

BANANA CINNAMON PANCAKES, P.36; OREO RICE BARS, P.88;
STEAK WITH CHIMICHURRI AND ROASTED SWEET POTATOES, P.118

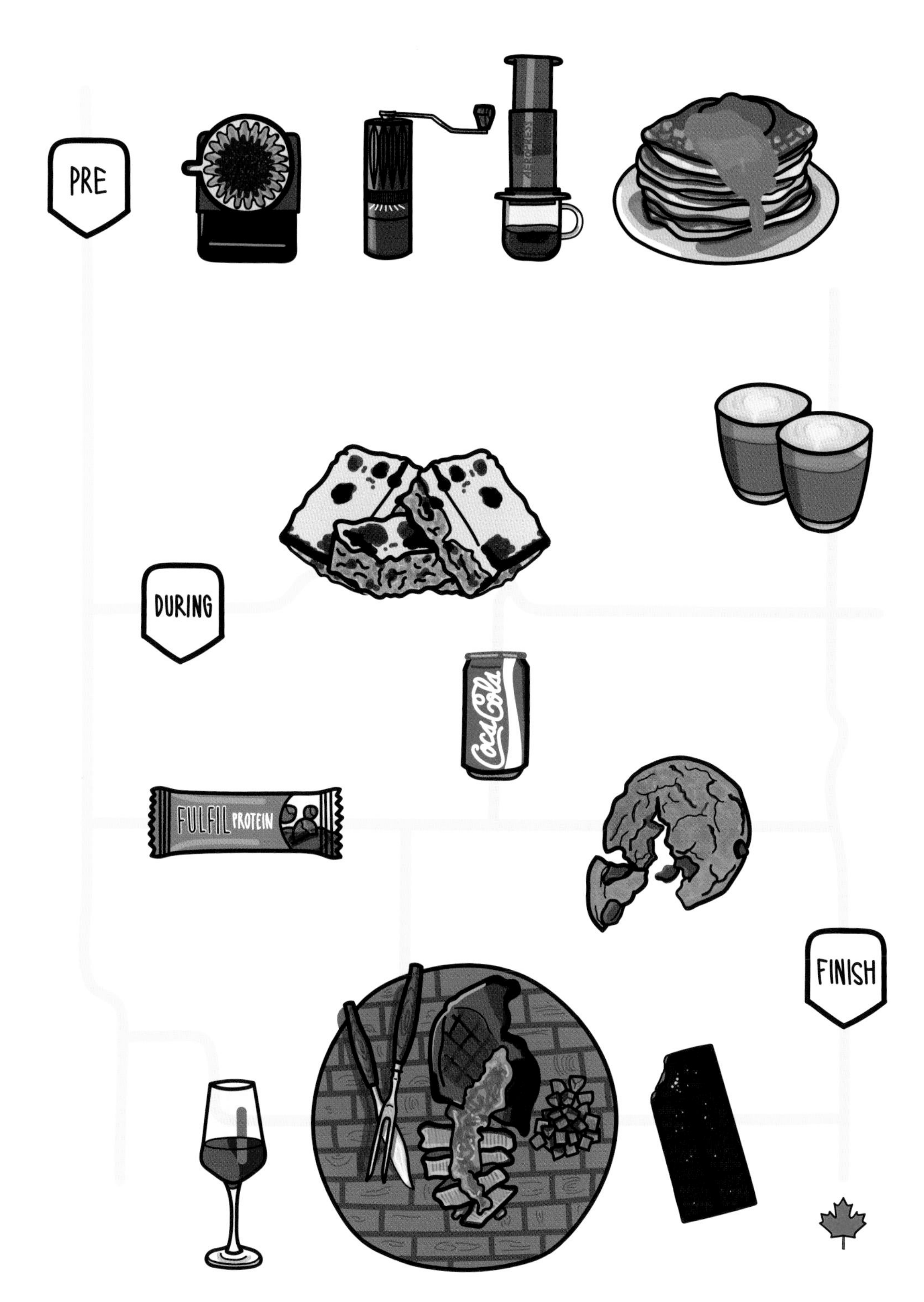
PRE
AEROPRESS
DURING
Coca-Cola
FULFIL PROTEIN
FINISH

BANANA CINNAMON PANCAKES

SERVES 1 HUNGRY PERSON OR 2 AS PART OF A BIGGER BREAKFAST

1 banana

1 egg plus 1 egg white, whisked together

1 tbsp maple syrup, plus extra for serving

70g plain flour (or oat or almond flour)

¼ tsp Himalayan pink sea salt

½ tsp cinnamon

¼ tsp ground cardamom

1 tbsp oil or butter for frying

almond butter for serving

maple syrup for serving

Pancakes may be the ultimate comfort breakfast and these provide that – along with power, thanks to almond butter, an extra egg and banana.

Mash the banana in a medium bowl.

Whisk in the egg, egg white and maple syrup, then sift in the flour, salt and spices.

Mix everything together lightly until smooth.

Heat the oil or butter in a frying pan over a medium heat. Drop 2–3 tablespoons of batter onto the pan to make a small pancake and fry in batches of one or two at a time.

Serve with the almond butter and a splash of maple syrup.

VARIATION

Apple Pancakes
Substitute 100g apple sauce for the banana. Shop-bought apple sauce is fine or, even better, make your own (see box).

Homemade apple sauce
Peel, core and chop 4 apples and place in a small saucepan with 25g brown sugar, 25ml water and 5ml apple cider vinegar. Simmer on low until the apple is soft, then mash gently with a fork. It will keep in the fridge for a week and also freezes well. It's delicious added to a cheese sandwich, or porridge – or a million other things.

LIZZY BANKS

AGE 30
UK

PROFESSIONAL RIDER

THE RIDE

A typical 3-hour training ride.

PRE-RIDE

Two large pieces of homemade sourdough **bread**, two **eggs**, usually scrambled, some kind of chutney or ketchup, a cup of Earl Grey tea and a glass of juice.

Then I'll usually get hungry again before I leave and have a couple of crumpets with some Marmite or another piece of bread and another cup of tea.

DURING

I would pack a Mars bar (cold weather only!), a banana, two good-sized, usually homemade bars – big, oaty **flapjack**-type things with honey and dried fruit or peel – or sometimes **roasted fresh coconut** (delicious) and a small pack of sweets like dolly mixture.

I usually start with two bottles of water with lemon squash and electrolyte powder and if I stop at a café, I'll get a piece of cake and a Coke.

POST-RIDE

Recovery drink immediately post ride, then... usually leftovers from the night before, so it's very variable. A big bowl of **mushroom risotto** with a good chunk of Parmesan, and salad with some meat, fish or eggs on the side. I am a big pasta fan so another option would be a big bowl of pasta: one of my easy go-to favourites post ride is a **carbonara**.

ADVICE

- I always take more food than I need for a ride, partly because I can't bear the thought of getting hungry, but also because I like to have a selection. I often find once I'm out riding that I fancy eating different things to what I wanted before I set off.

FAST AND EASY BREAD, P.41; PERFECT SCRAMBLED EGGS, P.40; OLD SCHOOL FLAPJACKS, P.86; ROASTED FRESH COCONUT, P.24, MUSHROOM RISOTTO, P.114; CARBONARA, P.113

EARL GREY
HOME MADE WITH LOVE
SOURDOUGH & EGGS
chutney
CRUMPETS & MARMITE
MARMITE
HUNGRY AGAIN
back pocket ride fuel
Mars
RECOVE
LEFTOVERS & CHILL.

PERFECT SCRAMBLED EGGS

SERVES 1

10g butter

2 large eggs

salt and freshly ground black pepper

a few sprigs of parsley or chives, chopped

These just-cooked buttery eggs are a great protein-rich start to the day. They're also fab in a Breakfast Burrito (p.64).

Gently melt the butter in a heavy-based pan over a medium heat. Meanwhile break the eggs into a medium bowl and beat them with a fork ('beat them like they owe you money' a chef once told me), then season the mix.

Add the egg mixture to the warm pan and, using a heat-proof spatula, pull the curds that are starting to cook at the edges of the pan into the centre. Be casual, don't overwork them. Let the curds form ribbons rather than bobbles, and keep the rhythm going until the second no liquid egg can be seen – approximately 2½ minutes. Slide the eggs straight onto your slices of freshly baked bread/ freshly made toast and sprinkle with the chopped fresh herbs.

VARIATION

Scrambled Tofu

Substitute 1 tbsp olive oil for the butter and 125g firm tofu for the eggs. Heat the oil in a heavy-based pan over a medium heat. Meanwhile crumble the tofu into a medium bowl and season well with salt, pepper and a pinch of turmeric. Add the mixture to the pan and heat for 5–7 minutes, stirring occasionally. Serve just like scrambled eggs, sprinkled with the fresh herbs.

FAST AND EASY BREAD

MAKES 3 SMALL LOAVES OF BREAD

1 tsp honey

7g (1 sachet) fast action dried yeast

450g plain white bread flour

¾ tsp fine sea salt

The beauty of this bread is that there is no special equipment or kneading required. Mix it quickly in a bowl and leave it to prove overnight (or for a couple of hours while you go for a cycle), then simply bake it and eat it warm.

Mix 60ml warm water with the honey and the sachet of yeast and leave to rest for 5 minutes. When you see a creamy Guinness-like 'head' starting to form and definite bubbling activity, it is ready to use.

Put the flour in a large bowl and make a well in the centre. Into that add the activated yeast mix and 340ml water, and stir well. Then add the salt and, using your hands or a spatula, mix everything together for a minute or so until it forms a dough.

Cover the bowl and set aside in a warmish place for a minimum of 2 hours, or overnight if you want fresh bread in the morning.

When you're ready to bake your bread, preheat the oven to 240°C/220°C fan. Line a large baking sheet with greaseproof paper and sprinkle with flour, then tip the dough out onto it. Using a knife, divide the dough into three equal loaves, leaving about 2cm between them, then sprinkle the tops with a little flour. The dough will be pretty wet so you won't be tempted to handle it too much. Bake for 30 minutes, or until the tops of the loaves are brown and the bottoms sound hollow when you tap them. Transfer to a wire rack to cool.

CHEESE AND APPLE QUINOA BITES

MAKES 12 SMALL BALLS

200g cooked quinoa (70g uncooked quinoa will yield 200g cooked)

1 apple, grated

90g Cheddar, grated

1 egg, beaten

olive oil for brushing

These are light, fresh tasting and so simple to make. Pre-cooked quinoa is sold in pouches and available in most supermarkets, or simply cook your own (see box).

Preheat your oven to 200°C/180°C fan.

In a large bowl, combine all the listed ingredients except the olive oil and stir thoroughly to combine.

Use your hands to form the mixture into balls that fit into the hollow of your palm and place on a baking tray.

Brush over the tops with a little olive oil.

Bake in the oven for 30 minutes, or until the balls are firm and a pale golden colour.

How to cook quinoa
Rinse 70g quinoa thoroughly under running water then tip into a saucepan with a decent pinch of salt and three times the amount of water (in this case 210ml).

Place over a medium heat and simmer, covered, for 15 minutes. It is cooked when the liquid has been absorbed and each grain shows a little white tail. Remove from the heat and fluff with a fork.

BUILDABLE SMOOTHIES

SERVES 1

TRY THESE:

Detoxing Triple Green
Water or apple juice, ginger, kale, spinach, banana, apple, kiwi, lemon juice to taste

Cleansing Cucumber and Mint
Water, chia, chard, alfalfa sprouts, cucumber, apple

Anti-Inflam Pineapple
Water, ice cubes, double spinach, pineapple, mango

Perfect for breakfast or as a snack, the beauty of the smoothie is that you can whizz it, slurp it and go. Start with the liquid as this creates a vortex, then add at least one item from each of the categories below and make sure everything is thoroughly blended. If you don't have a high-powered jug blender, a stick blender works fine too.

1. Start with 300–400ml **Liquid** such as water, coconut water, any of your favourite milks, apple juice (watch out for sugar in this), beetroot juice.

2. Add 2–4 tbsp **Supplements and Sweeteners** such as dates, honey, ginger, vanilla, raw cacao powder, cinnamon, nutmeg, maca, spirulina, matcha, protein powders.

3. Add 2 handfuls **Greens** such as spinach, kale, chard, baby gem, alfalfa sprouts (any tough stems and stalks removed).

4. Add 1–3 tbsp **Healthy Fats** such as avocado, chia, flax seeds, yoghurt, tofu, nut or seed butter.

5. Add 2 handfuls fresh or frozen **Fruits and Veggies** such as bananas, berries, peaches, cherries, mango, pineapple, cucumber, cooked sweet potato.

KITTY'S MIX

400ml almond milk
4 dates (1½ tbsp honey)
2 tsp maca
1 tsp spirulina, if you have it
1 scoop chocolate or vanilla protein powder
1 tbsp almond butter
1 large banana

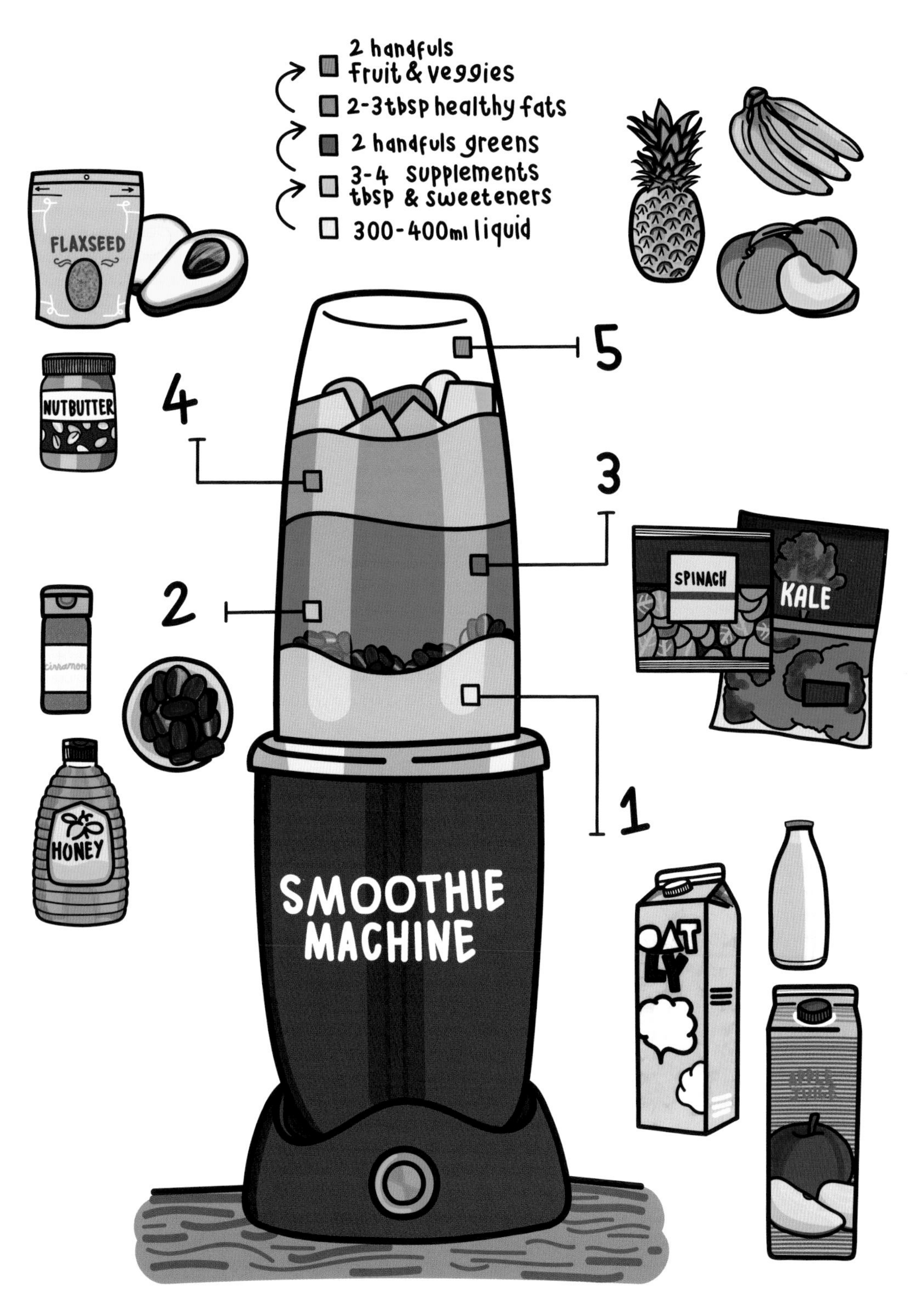

2 handfuls fruit & veggies
2-3tbsp healthy fats
2 handfuls greens
3-4 tbsp supplements & sweeteners
300-400ml liquid
FLAXSEED
NUTBUTTER
HONEY
SPINACH
KALE
5
4
3
2
1
SMOOTHIE MACHINE

VICTORIA GILL

AGE 40
WINCHESTER, UK

ROAD RIDER AND TIME TRIALIST

Enjoys solo exploring (known to others as getting lost), time-trial racing, occasional coffee and caking.

THE RIDE

A pre-race reccy ride the day before the National 100-mile Time Trial Championships. Multi-lap, decent weather, fair course. (Oh, and I won!)

Breakfast: strong black coffee and **raspberry baked oats** (porridge with its lucky race pants on) made with oat milk, mashed banana, frozen raspberries and honey, and topped with nuts and seeds. (Stealth carbs tip: adding a mashed banana and honey to the baked oats ramps up the carbs without adding bulk.)

Snack: coffee shop stop for an oat milk flat white and a homemade cake (Bakewell slice is my current fave).

Lunch: **chicken salad with mango, pomegranate and quinoa topped with salted cashews**. It's sweet and salty so ticks all the macro and taste boxes, and it's feel-good food and moreish, meaning you will eat enough even if you have a touch of pre-race-day nerves. I made an extra portion for my post-race Tupperware lunch.

Snack: two fun-size Milky Ways – just because!

Dinner: a **green risotto** with grilled salmon – it's high carb, easy to digest and familiar.

Dessert: Greek yoghurt and berries.

ADVICE

- Carbs are king! What you eat the day before a big ride is as important (if not more so!) as what you eat on the day itself.
- Fuel ahead. You'll be blitzing through the cals on race day so it's critical to your success to start with a full tank. You've done the hard work; don't let poor fuelling let you down.
- Fun calories = energy legs. Eat that damn cake!
- Eat familiar foods. You don't want an enforced mid-ride pit stop in the bushes. This is not fun or glamorous.

RASPBERRY BAKED OATS, P.51; BUILDABLE SALADS, P.102; SPRING RISOTTO, P.115

2. GOOD SLEEP

3. 100-MILE TIME TRIAL

APRICOT HEAVEN GRANOLA BARS

MAKES 12 BARS

120g pecans

190g plain flour

120g rolled oats

65g caster sugar

85g soft brown sugar

½ tsp sea salt

½ tsp bicarbonate of soda

170g butter, melted

250g apricot jam

These bars don't require a ton of ingredients and the jam in the centre makes them moist and zingy. You could substitute other types of jam – I've used rhubarb and ginger before and they were knock out. Lemon curd would also be excellent.

Preheat the oven to 180°C/160°C fan and line a 20 x 20cm baking tin with greaseproof paper.

Place the pecans, flour, oats, sugars, salt and bicarbonate of soda in a large bowl and mix well, then add the melted butter, stirring everything together until well coated.

Put two thirds of the mixture into the lined baking tin, making sure it's evenly spread out to the corners. Press the mixture down into the tin. A potato masher can be useful for a job like this, but clean hands are just as good.

Add the apricot jam and spread it all over the base. Now add the rest of the buttery oat and pecan mixture and use the tips of your fingers to spread it evenly across the surface.

Bake for about 40 minutes, or until the top is golden and it smells irresistible (resist though: hot jam is like molten lava).

Allow to cool a little, then cut into 12 bars.

BLUEBERRY AND WALNUT BAKED OATS

MAKES 12 BARS

240g rolled oats (not instant oats)

120g soft brown sugar

150g walnuts, chopped

1 tsp baking powder

1 tsp cinnamon

½ tsp salt

2 large eggs, beaten

250ml milk, whichever type you prefer

1 tsp vanilla extract

120g blueberries, frozen or fresh

1 tbsp brown sugar for sprinkling over top (optional)

If, like Lizzy Banks, you just don't like porridge, this breakfast is going to be your best friend. It has all the health benefits of porridge plus eggs for a protein boost. It's easily customisable and, what's more, it's portable. That's a win.

Preheat the oven to 180°C/160°C fan. Line a 20 x 20cm baking tin with greaseproof paper.

In a large bowl, combine the oats, sugar, walnuts, baking powder, cinnamon and salt.

In a separate bowl, whisk together the eggs, milk and vanilla. Add the egg mixture to the bowl with the dry ingredients and mix well, then fold in the blueberries, reserving a handful to sprinkle on top. Pour the mixture into the prepared baking tin, top with the blueberries and sprinkle with the brown sugar, if using.

Bake for 40 minutes, or until golden and firm to the touch. Allow to cool a little before cutting into bars.

VARIATIONS

Raspberry Baked Oats
Omit the cinnamon and substitute 100g shelled, unsalted pistachios for the walnuts and stir through either 150g Raspberry Compote (p.144) or frozen raspberries instead of the blueberries.

Cherry, Chocolate and Coconut Baked Oats
Omit the cinnamon and substitute 150g fresh or frozen pitted cherries for the blueberries and add 100g chocolate chips and 100g unsweetened desiccated coconut.

EMMA BENTLEY

AGE 30
LONDON, UK

ROAD RIDER

Enjoys multi-discipline racing, adventure sports and being outdoors.

THE RIDE

Crystal Palace Crits, London (45 minutes). A 'crit' or criterium, is a circuit race of a specified number of laps which takes place on a closed course.

The great thing about mid-week crits is that, if you're a midweek worker, you don't get much time to overthink them. People often ride straight from work to the event.

PRE-RIDE

At lunchtime, I'll make sure I've had more than a salad (but usually just a sandwich and a coconut bar) and make sure I've had some water. After work, I'll ride down to Cadence in Crystal Palace for sign-on about an hour before the start. I'll grab a little espresso from the café as a post-work pick-me-up, drink some more water and have a little Tupperware of veggie pasta. We'll roll down to the park to watch what's left of the previous races and get sorted. Ten minutes before the start, I'll have a gel if I've remembered to pack one. Crystal Palace is pretty explosive, which doesn't come that naturally to me, so I need all the help I can get there!

POST-RIDE

After the race, normal thoughts of recovery usually go out the window in place of beer, pizza and great chat.

RACE
RACE SIGN ON
NAME NO. CLUB SIGNED
EMMA 12 5THFLOOR
CRYSTAL PALACE CRITS
GEL
Ride to race
Ride home
OFFICE LUNCH
LATE DINNER
LONDONS BEST PIZZA
Santa Maria
Pizzeria
CANOPY
LONDON IPA
CANOPY
LONDON IPA

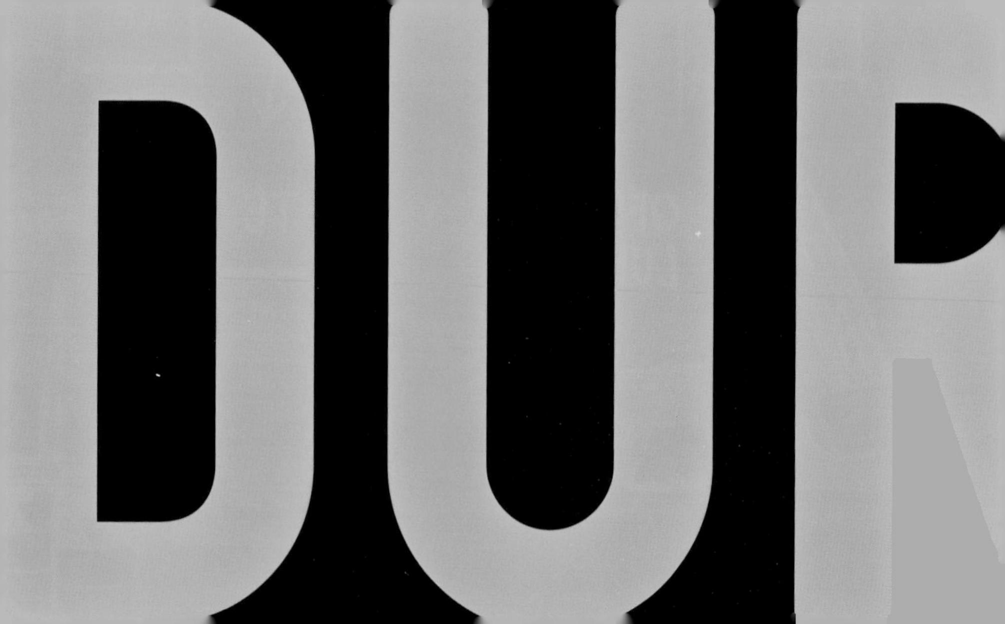
DUR

The two basic components to remember when you're out on a ride are hydration and carbohydrates. Don't go anywhere without a water bottle (or two), especially for a longer ride, and critically if the temperatures are warm. And whatever you tuck into your back pockets or bar bag, allow for a small carb snack roughly every 30 minutes of your journey. For a short ride, Sweet Potato Falafels with Tahini Dressing (p.78) in a wrap, Energy Balls (p.94) or a banana would all do perfectly and are easy to stow away. Additionally, don't overlook the value of a snack containing protein such as nut butter to provide an energy boost. If your route is long and intense, space becomes a consideration and gels can come into their own.

DURING STAR FOODS

For cyclists, bananas are magical things. They contain tryptophan, a protein that the body converts into serotonin, known to relax you, improve your mood and generally make you feel happier. They also contain essential carbs for energy, an amino acid called tyrosine which has been proven to enhance alertness and ability to focus, vitamin B6 which regulates blood glucose levels, potassium (which is depleted when you sweat), protein and lots of fibre. What's more, they come pre-packed in biodegradable packaging, are easy to peel and really easy to store in a jersey pocket.

SWEET POTATOES

The sweet potato is a nutritional all-star. It is jam-packed with vitamins, in particular A, C and E, as well as beta carotene, protein, fibre and carbohydrates. But, it's the versatility of the sweet potato that truly gives it supersta status. It's delicious baked or as chips and it makes fantastic, fudgy brownies. A smart idea is to bake or steam 3–4 sweet potatoes at the start of the week and keep them in your fridge ready to make into falafels for the road, or to add to smoothies or a quick nutritious salad when you get home.

NUT BUTTERS

These days it's not just peanuts that come in spreadable paste form; you can buy almond, cashew and walnut butters too. Protein-rich and nutrient dense, they provid concentrated energy and flavour, so it's no wonder they feature in so many cyclists' food diaries.

When choosing nut butters, select brands with as few added ingredients as possible, and avoid any with added stabilisers, palm oil, hydrogenated oils and corn syrup or other sugars. Nut butters pack a lot of nutrition into a little food, which is handy for quashing hunger without filling you up, but each of them brings its own extra benefits:

- Peanut butter is highest in protein – but it is a legume and an allergen, so be careful if you're helping out a bonking friend.

- Almond butter is highest in vitamin E and also rich in calcium.

- Cashew butter isn't one of the nutritional forerunners but it is rich in magnesium and copper.

- Walnut butter is highest in Omega 3 fatty acids.

- Sunflower seed butter is a good alternative if you have nut allergies. It is lower in fat but still rich in zinc, iron, vitamin E and magnesium.

STAY HYDRATED

For a ride of less than 60 minutes, aim to have two or three sips from your water bottle every 10–15 minutes. Make your water more delicious by adding a slice of lemon, a wedge of cucumber or a sprig of mint.

For rides longer than 60 minutes, look to supplement your water with a tablet for electrolytes and carbs, or replace it with a sports drink so that you replace minerals you lose through sweating (or make your own, see box). Recent studies have shown that after 90 minutes of cycling, women process 25% more carbohydrates from a sports drink than men, so consider this advantage on longer rides.

DIY ELECTROLYTE SPORTS DRINKS

It's easy to make your own sports drink. Here are two cost-effective versions that will help to keep you hydrated:

- 500ml water + 500ml fruit juice + ¼ tsp sea salt
- 500ml water + juice of ½ lemon + 2 tsp honey + ¼ tsp sea salt

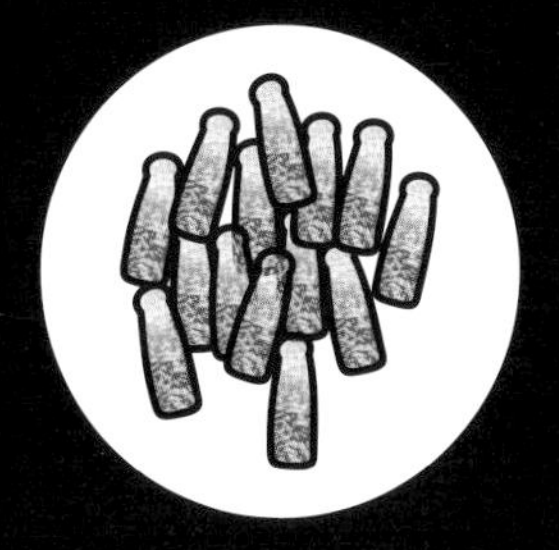

AVOID A BONK

Plan for a small carb snack every 30–45 minutes when cycling. This could consist of a banana, 3–4 Medjool dates, 15 dried apricots or 2 handfuls of raisins or, alternatively, 2 handfuls of gummy bears or a big handful of cola bottles.

GELS

If you take gels for energy, it's crucial to up your water intake. Gels boost energy but have a very low water content, so compensate for this by drinking more water; otherwise they can sit heavily in your stomach and may cause nausea.

VEDANGI KULKARNI

Likes long-distance adventure rides with overnight stays.

AGE 22
DORSET, UK

ROAD RIDER

THE RIDE

A 100km ride in the rolling hills of South West England.

PRE-RIDE

Coffee. A big bowl of muesli with milk, to which I added banana, strawberries, raspberries, blackberries, blueberries, kiwi, grapes and some seeds.

DURING

Outdoor Provisions bars (Kendal Mint Choc and Cherry Bakewell), a **veggie wrap** (cucumber, tomato, rocket, jalapeños, olives and pepper) with sweet chilli sauce, garlic mayo and Nando's Lemon and Herb sauce. And, of course, peanut butter – lots of peanut butter, right out of the jar from my food pouch. Coffee from a flask.

POST-RIDE

Avocado and **scrambled eggs** on **bread** with peanut butter spread on the top of it. Andddd hot chocolate. Always hot chocolate!

ADVICE

- If you stop for a food break during the ride, layer up before you set off again, especially if it's night-time.
- You'll never regret carrying a flask of warm tea or coffee on a cold day out on the bike.

BUILDABLE WRAPS, P.68; PERFECT SCRAMBLED EGGS, P.40; FAST AND EASY BREAD, P.41

LOTS OF

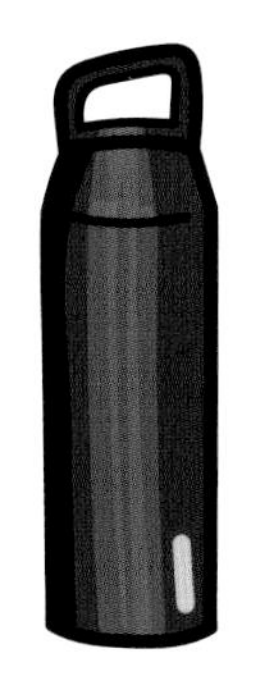

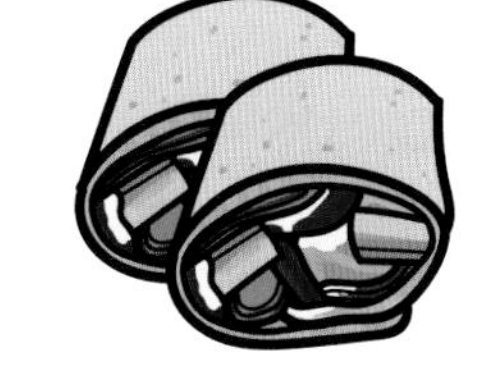

BUTTER

PREP 15MIN
COOK 5MIN

BREAKFAST BURRITO

SERVES 1

for the pico de gallo

4 plum tomatoes, chopped

2 spring onions, finely chopped

large handful of coriander, chopped

½ a mild red chilli such as Serrano, or to your taste

juice of ½ lime

1 garlic clove, finely chopped

sea salt to taste

for the burrito

1 large tortilla or wrap

1 quantity Perfect Scrambled Eggs (p.40)

½ red pepper, chopped or sliced

20–30g Cheddar, grated

Zesty, fresh pico de gallo gives the eggs in this a feisty kick. Don't be tempted to overfill it and create an out-of-control monster burrito – this is one of those times when you really do have to follow your head over your heart.

To make the pico de gallo, simply combine the tomatoes, spring onions, coriander, chilli, lime juice, garlic and salt in a bowl and mix.

Place the tortilla in a dry frying pan and soften it by heating it for about 30 seconds on each side, then transfer it to a flat surface such as a chopping board. To assemble the burrito, layer the scrambled eggs, red pepper and grated cheese in the centre and spoon over as much pico de gallo as desired. First fold in the sides, then fold the bottom edge up over the filling and tuck it under it. Finally, roll the burrito away from you to make a nice leakproof parcel. Get it ready to pack by wrapping it tightly in foil. The trick is not to go mad with the filling.

Pico de gallo can be prepared in advance and stored in the fridge.

It doesn't need to be just scrambled eggs in the burrito; feel free to add slices of smoked streaky bacon, sautéed mushrooms or fried onions. Anything goes.

QUESADILLA

SERVES 1

1 tsp sunflower oil

1 large tortilla or wrap

25g meltable cheese such as Gruyère or Cheddar, grated

100g refried beans

small handful of coriander, chopped

1 spring onion, finely chopped

You can customise this versatile Mexican grilled cheese by adding anything you fancy, from pesto to mango chutney. Here, the refried beans add a wonderful texture and make it just a bit more substantial. The half-moon shape holds the filling neatly and also fits conveniently in a jersey back pocket.

Gently heat the sunflower oil in a heavy-based frying pan big enough to hold the tortilla.

Place the tortilla in the frying pan and heat it for about 30 seconds on each side, until it is warm. While still in the pan, scatter half the cheese, then the beans, coriander and spring onion and finally the remaining cheese over half of the tortilla. Fold the empty half over the filling and gently flatten it down with a spatula. Fry on that side for 2–3 minutes, then carefully flip over to cook the other side for the same amount of time.

The tortilla should be golden brown and the cheese melted. Allow to cool before wrapping.

You can buy refried beans in tins or, alternatively, simply fry half a tin (200g) of drained and rinsed borlotti or kidney beans in some olive oil, finely chopped garlic and ½ tsp paprika for 5 minutes, then crush using a potato masher or blitz in a food processor.

BUILDABLE WRAPS

TRY THESE:

Mexican
Large crispy iceberg lettuce leaves stuffed with Mexican-style cooked rice, pico de gallo, sour cream and grated Cheddar.

Classic
Leftover roast chicken, watercress, vine tomatoes, wholegrain mustard and mayo.

Kitty's Wrap
Fresh blueberries and peanut butter.

Simple to make and easily tucked into a bar bag or pocket, wraps in all their forms are a hungry cyclist's best friend. Keep them healthy if you want, fill them with Nutella and marshmallows if you know you're going to need a boost, use leftovers if you're feeling thrifty. Whatever your filling, soften your tortilla first by heating it quickly in a microwave or in a dry frying pan. Consider texture and flavour distribution, and try not to overfill.

1. Start with a **Base** such as steamed salmon, Sweet Potato Falafels (p.78), leftover roast chicken, Roasted Sweet Potatoes (p.118), thinly sliced steak, grilled prawns, seared halloumi, dahl, your favourite cheese, cooked quinoa (p.44) or rice.

2. Add **Greens** such as crispy iceberg lettuce, baby spinach, watercress, cavolo nero, pea shoots, rocket or bean sprouts.

3. Add **Veggies** such as avocado, red pepper, grated carrot, vine tomatoes, cucumber; **Fruit** such as sliced apples, slices of mango, thinly sliced fresh pineapple.

4. Add flavour **Boosters** such as Pico de Gallo (p.64), fresh herbs, pumpkin seeds, finely sliced radishes, a squeeze of lime juice, homemade pickles, chilli flakes, orange zest, salty roasted peanuts, olives.

VIETNAMESE SUMMER ROLL

Rice paper, grilled prawns sprinkled with fresh lime juice, red pepper, finely chopped lettuce and coriander.

step 1 BASE
e.g. chicken, salmon, steak halloumi, rice.
step 2 GREENS
e.g. lettuce, spinach, rocket, peashoots.
step 3 VEGGIES & FRUIT
e.g. avocado, apple, tomatoes, mango.
step 4 BOOSTERS
e.g. herbs, seeds, peanuts, chilli flakes.
THAT'S A WRAP!

SHUHENA ISLAM

AGE 30
LONDON, UK

ROAD RIDER

Likes long distance rides and group riding; a weekend warrior.

THE RIDE

80–160km weekend ride/ sportive – pace depends on route, and which friends/club mates I am out with.

PRE-RIDE

Usually black coffee and toast. If it's a sportive, I have oats with peanut butter and jam – a real breakfast of champions! I always prep my bidons the night before with water and SiS hydration tablets and stick them in the fridge.

DURING

I fry samosas before I leave – I loved having my tiffin of Bangladeshi fried treats on the top of Box Hill! Everyone thought I had a three-course meal. I remember taking a paratha to Ride London and it flying out of my top tube bag! It's important to fuel on rides and you eat more if you enjoy the food.

I carry Clif chocolate chip bars in my jersey pocket but I can't resist eating them before I start my ride. I also carry SiS gels and halal Haribos, fizzy bottles and candy kittens just in case I bonk – or someone else in the squad does.

If we cycle to the beach, fish and chips are mandatory, though I did enjoy a cheeky shawarma in Brighton!

POST-RIDE

If I'm naughty, I pick up grilled wings and chips locally and sneak them upstairs whilst I upload my ride to Strava. I love my mum's homemade rice and curry, and if she's made biryani, I could quite possibly go to food heaven and coma simultaneously after a ride!

ADVICE

- Even if I ride at 5am, I make sure I eat. You can't go into a ride hungry, so eat cereal bars, fruit, Nutella toast – anything you can nibble.
- Eat every hour. Learn to eat and drink on the bike or at least hydrate at traffic lights, or where it's safe to do so.

CHEAT'S SAMOSA WITH SPICED POTATO AND PEAS, P.73

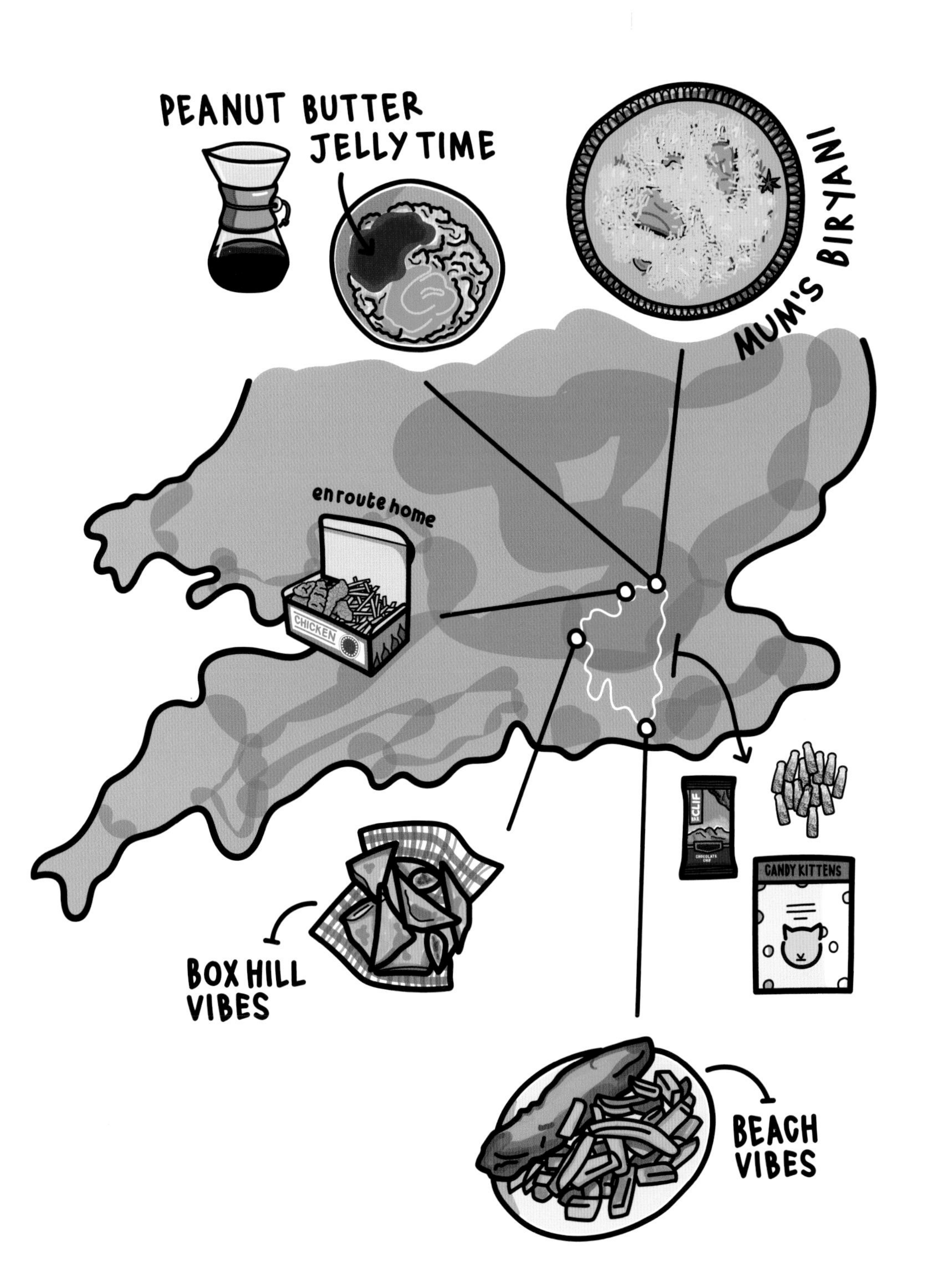
PEANUT BUTTER
JELLY TIME
MUM'S BIRYANI
en route home
CHICKEN
CLIF
CANDY KITTENS
BOX HILL
VIBES
BEACH
VIBES

CHEAT'S SAMOSA WITH SPICED POTATO AND PEAS

MAKES 2 SAMOSAS

200g potatoes (about 2 medium potatoes) such as Rooster, Desiree or King Edward, washed but not peeled, chopped into 1cm cubes

salt

2 tsp good-quality curry paste

zest and juice of 1/4 lemon

30g frozen garden peas or petit pois

salt and freshly ground black pepper

2 large tortillas or wraps

a few slices of cucumber

small handful of coriander

This makes enough filling for two samosas, which will make a satisfying lunch – any leftovers will keep in the fridge for 3 days and make an excellent snack.

Bring the potatoes to the boil in a pan of salted cold water and boil until tender, about 10 minutes. Drain the potatoes and, in a bowl, mix them with the curry paste, lemon zest and juice and the peas. The peas will quickly defrost when mixed with the hot potatoes. Finally, season to taste. This is the spiced potato and pea 'samosa' filling.

Place a wrap in a dry frying pan and soften it by heating it for about 30 seconds on each side. Then place the warm tortilla on a board and make a cut from the centre of the tortilla to the bottom between the empty quarter and the coriander edge. Work clockwise in quarters: leave the first quarter empty, fill the second with half of the filling, the third with cucumber slices and the fourth with coriander. Fold the unfilled quarter of tortilla over the potato, then fold the potato mix over the cucumber and, finally, fold the cucumber over the coriander, so you have a samosa-shaped triangle. Repeat the process with the other tortilla, then wrap and go.

SCANDINAVIAN-STYLE SEED BREAD

MAKES 1 LOAF

- 75g sunflower seeds
- 60g pumpkin seeds
- 90g flax seeds or linseeds
- 2 tsp coriander or fennel seeds (optional)
- 75g hazelnuts or almonds, skins on
- 145g rolled oats
- 2 tbsp chia seeds
- 4 tbsp psyllium seed husks or 3 tbsp psyllium husk powder
- 1 tsp sea salt or ½ tsp ordinary table salt
- 1 tbsp honey
- 3 tbsp olive oil

This is my interpretation of a fantastic recipe from Sarah Britton of *My New Roots*. It's wholegrain, gluten-free, full of fibre and completely delicious. Try adding spice seeds for a real pop of flavour. This is so dense that a decent slice is almost like a savoury granola bar.

Line a 2lb (approximately 23 x 13 x 7cm) loaf tin with greaseproof paper.

In a large bowl, combine the sunflower seeds, pumpkin seeds, flax or linseeds, coriander or fennel seeds (if using), hazelnuts or almonds, rolled oats, chia seeds, psyllium seed husks or powder and salt, and stir well. Whisk the honey, olive oil and 350ml warm water together in a measuring cup. Add this to the dry ingredients and mix well until incorporated and the dough is very thick. (If too thick to stir, add 1–2 teaspoons of water until it is manageable.)

Tip the dough into the lined loaf tin and smooth out the top with the back of a spoon. Cover loosely with a tea towel and leave to rest on the counter for at least 2 hours, or a full day or night. It does not need to be refrigerated.

When ready to bake the bread, preheat your oven to 180°C/160°C fan. Bake the bread on the middle rack for 20 minutes. Then take it out of the oven, remove the loaf tin and put it back in the oven upside down and directly on the rack. Bake for another 30–40 minutes. The bread is done when it sounds hollow when tapped. Allow it to cool completely before slicing. The bread will keep in an airtight container for up to 5 days and also freezes well.

SOPHIE EDMONDSON

AGE 33
LONDON, UK

ROAD AND OFF-ROAD RIDER

Enjoys short sharp races, big days out on tarmac or ridgeways, weekend wild camps; always in fresh air, ideally riding somewhere with sun-dappled sunlight through beautiful trees.

THE RIDE

200km off-road race, Sussex Mystery Tour – a one-day self-supported route on the South Downs, England.

PRE-RIDE

Peanut butter and strawberry jam on rye bread. The plan was a **flapjack** in lieu of oats, but I was camping and woke up hungry so went with my mid-morning ride snack instead (which was wrapped in beeswax cloth). A tip is not to cut your sandwich so it stays flat and together in your pocket/bike bag.

DURING

Trek bars (dense but perfectly sized dairy-free flapjacks topped with dark chocolate), oat milk flat white atop Ditchling Beacon, eight-piece **falafel** with wedges and wrap for lunch and finally a DIY bag of trail mix with dates, almonds, Brazil nuts and dried figs.

POST-RIDE

Homemade vegan pizza (potato with rosemary and vegan mozzarella) made in an outdoor oven, fuelled with wood chips. To end, a handful of M&Ms.

ADVICE

- For hot summer rides, a pinch of salt in your water bottle with some cordial and a sprig of mint is ace refreshment.
- For winter rides, mix whisky-soaked fruit or mincemeat into flapjacks or rice cakes for some extra warming properties!
- Try to hydrate before arriving at a café stop; that way you don't confuse hunger with dehydration and don't roll away feeling really thirsty but too full to top up with liquid.

OLD SCHOOL FLAPJACKS, P.86; SWEET POTATO FALAFELS AND TAHINI DRESSING, P.78

ADVICE bees wax cloth.
ADVICE don't cut in half.
MORNING CAMPERS
ALL HAIL DIY TRAIL
TREK
COCOA OAT
ditchling beacon

SWEET POTATO FALAFELS AND TAHINI DRESSING

SERVES 4

for the sweet potato falafels

about 2 medium sweet potatoes (500g baked flesh)

50g gram flour (chickpea flour)

½ tsp baking powder

1 garlic glove, finely chopped

1½ tsp ground cumin

1½ tsp ground coriander

¼ tsp sea salt

handful of coriander, finely chopped

juice and zest of ½ lemon

50ml olive oil

20g sesame seeds

Although you may have to make a pitstop to eat them, these falafels are perfect for a cycling lunch because they're satisfying without being heavy, and the lemon zest and coriander give them an enjoyable freshness. This makes more than you need for one pitta so make a batch and freeze them.

Preheat the oven to 200°C/180°C fan. Place the sweet potatoes on the top shelf of the oven and bake for approximately 50 minutes, until soft. When cool enough to handle, cut the sweet potatoes in half, scoop out the flesh and discard the skins.

Mash the cooked sweet potato in a large bowl, then add the rest of the ingredients, except for the olive oil and sesame seeds. Mix well, then chill in the fridge for 30 minutes.

Preheat the oven to 200°C/180°C fan. Line a baking tray with greaseproof paper and drizzle with half the olive oil. Using two tablespoons, arrange 12 evenly sized balls of the mixture on a baking tray and sprinkle the sesame seeds over them. Drizzle the rest of the olive oil over the falafels and bake for 15–20 minutes, then turn over and bake for a further 15 minutes, or until the seeds are brown and the exterior of the falafels is crispy.

for the tahini dressing

1 garlic clove, finely chopped

juice of ½ lemon

100g tahini

pinch of sea salt

pinch of cumin

to serve

4 pittas or wraps

4 handfuls of salad leaves

2 vine tomatoes, sliced

¼ cucumber, sliced

To make the tahini dressing, put all the ingredients in a medium bowl along with 6 tablespoons water and whisk well until combined. Serve three falafels in a warmed pitta bread or tortilla wrap, with salad leaves, tomato and cucumber slices and a drizzle of tahini dressing.

Wrap tightly in greaseproof paper and/or tin foil.

SWEET POTATO BROWNIES

MAKES 12

- 1 medium sweet potato (250g baked flesh)
- 115g peanut or almond butter, microwaved for 10–15 seconds to soften it
- 1 tsp vanilla extract
- 150ml maple syrup
- 50g plain flour
- 50g cacao powder
- 80g dark chocolate chips
- 1½ tsp bicarbonate of soda
- ¼ tsp sea salt

This brownie is the perfect combination of rich, chocolatey intensity without being too dense and sticky. The protein-rich nut butter provides the oil, and the starchy sweet potato binds everything together. As well as being high in fibre, sweet potatoes contain antioxidants and vitamins A, C and B6. It's a sweet vegan miracle, naturally.

Preheat your oven to 190°C/170°C fan. Place your sweet potato on the top shelf and bake for approximately 45 minutes, until soft. When cool enough to handle, cut in half, scoop out the flesh and discard the skin. Turn your oven down to 180°C/160°C fan and line a 20 x 20cm baking tin with greaseproof paper.

In a large bowl, use a hand mixer to mix the sweet potato, peanut or almond butter, vanilla extract and maple syrup until it is smooth and really well incorporated, about 2 minutes.

In a separate bowl, combine the flour, cacao powder, chocolate chips, bicarbonate of soda and salt and mix well to combine.

Stir the dry ingredients into the wet, then transfer into the prepared baking tin, spreading the mixture to the corners of the tin. Bake for 20 minutes, until the top is set and there's only a slight wobble when you shake the pan. It will set as it cools. When cool, cut into bars. These keep for a week wrapped in greaseproof paper and will retain their moistness.

HANNAH BARNES

AGE 27
ENGLAND, UK

PROFESSIONAL ROAD RIDER

THE RIDE
Weekly 2–3 hour training ride.

PRE-RIDE
A bowl of chocolate Weetabix minis, a banana and one slice of toast with raspberry jam and cheese.

DURING
I'll have a homemade **flapjack** 30 minutes into my ride. I start my efforts at 45 minutes and after the second and fourth effort I have a SiS gel (vanilla flavour). After the efforts I'll have a stroopwafel and ride home. To drink, I always carry two bottles with Robinsons tropical squash.

POST-RIDE
Two slices of toast with avocado, eggs and smoked salmon.

OLD SCHOOL FLAPJACKS, P.86

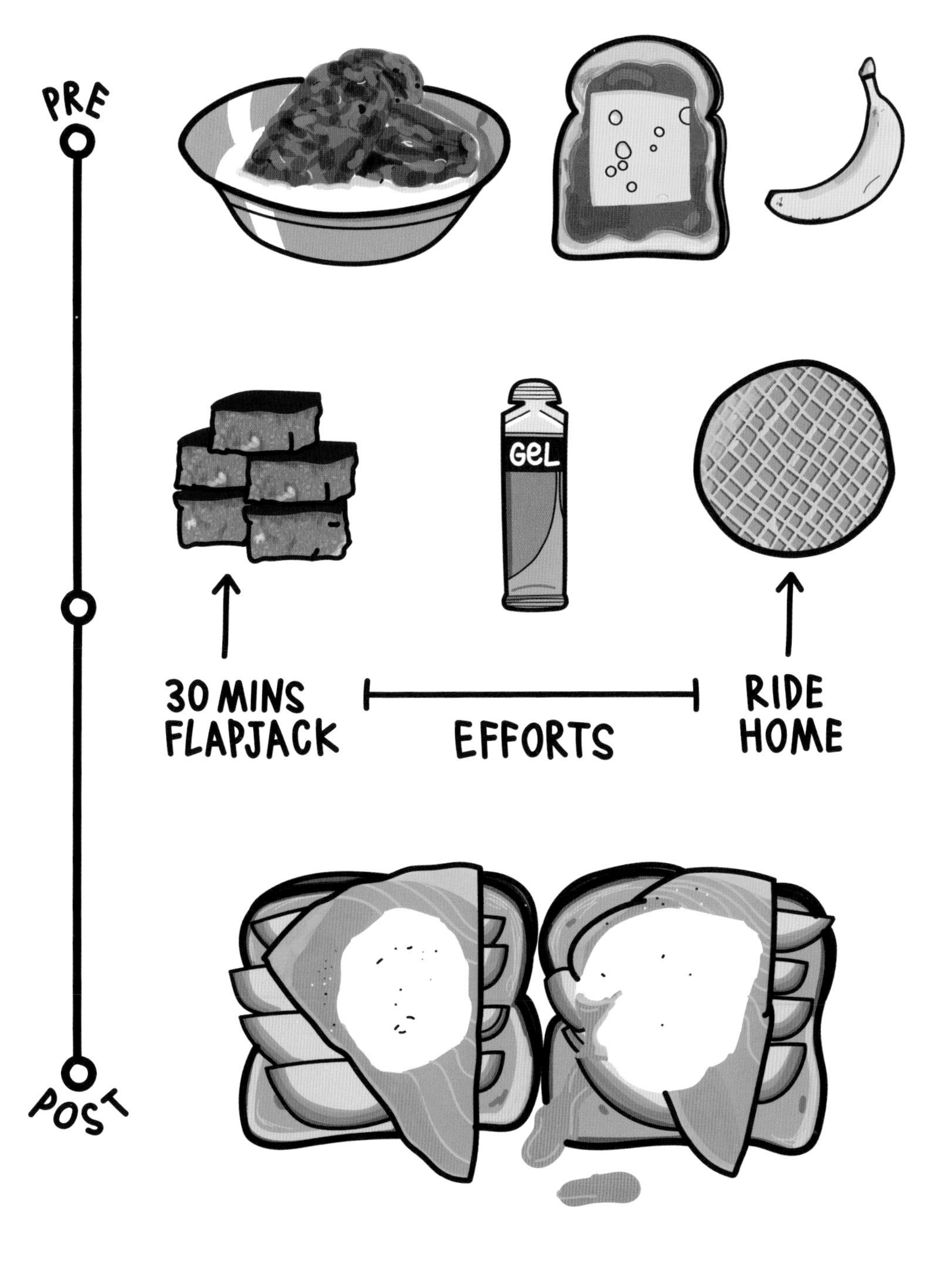
PRE
GEL
30 MINS
FLAPJACK
EFFORTS
RIDE
HOME
POST

OLD SCHOOL FLAPJACKS

MAKES 12

125g butter

85g soft brown sugar

85g golden syrup

200g quick cook oats (such as Scott's Porridge Oats or Quaker oats)

¼ tsp sea salt

This is the unadorned old school recipe scribbled in a million kitchen notebooks across the land. It's also the original energy bar, easily wrapped in greaseproof (or a hanky in the old days) and stuffed in a pocket. Simple, comforting, tasty and always standing by.

Preheat the oven to 180°C/160°C fan and line a 20 x 20cm baking tin with greaseproof paper.

In a medium pan, melt the butter with the sugar and the golden syrup, stirring from time to time.

Add the oats and salt, and stir well, until all the oats are coated in the buttery syrup.

Transfer the mixture to the baking tin, and pat down so it's right into the corners and the surface is flat and even.

Bake for 20 minutes, until lightly golden all over. Remove from the oven and cool for about 10 minutes before slicing into bars.

VARIATIONS

Honey and Apricot Flapjacks
Substitute honey for the golden syrup and add 85g chopped dried apricots to the mixture before baking.

Ginger and Chocolate Flapjacks
Add 80g crystallised ginger, chopped into 1cm pieces, and 80g good-quality dark chocolate, chopped into 1cm chunks, to the mixture before baking.

OREO RICE BARS

MAKES 12 SMALL BARS

150g short grain rice such as sushi rice, pudding rice or Arborio

200ml unsweetened coconut milk, stirred well so cream is incorporated

½ tsp Himalayan pink salt

1 packet Oreo cookies (roughly 20)

This is a bonk buster of a recipe inspired by Alison Jackson. It is essentially a set coconut rice pudding heavily laced with Oreo cookies. I can imagine gaining power just knowing it's in my bar bag. Note that it must be stored in the fridge.

Line a 20 x 20cm baking tin with greaseproof paper.

Rinse the rice in several changes of water until it runs clear. This is important to rid the rice of excess starch that can make it stodgy rather than fluffy. Place in a medium saucepan and add the coconut milk, 160ml water and the salt. Stir to combine.

Bring to a quick boil, then pop on the lid, reduce the heat to its lowest setting and let the rice simmer/steam for 20 minutes. Stir occasionally to ensure the rice is not sticking to the bottom of the pan.

Whilst the rice is cooking, either pulse the Oreos to a fine rubble consistency in a food processor, or put them in a sturdy, clear plastic bag and wallop them with a rolling pin to break them up.

When the rice is cooked, fluff it with a fork, then stir in the cookie rubble. Mix well, then tip the mixture into the prepared baking tin and smooth into an even layer.

Allow to cool in the tray for 15 minutes, then cut into bars and wrap individually in greaseproof paper. Store for up to 3 days in the fridge, ready to grab and go.

JANE DENNYSON

AGE 45
GULLANE, SCOTLAND

ROAD RIDER

Enjoys long-distance riding – single and multi-day events.

THE RIDE

A 300km audax called 'Alston & back' which starts in Galashiels in the Scottish Borders and heads south, past Gretna, over the English border to a town called Alston – and back.

PRE-RIDE

Porridge made with oats, water, a pinch of salt and almonds. (I soak it overnight, then heat it up in the microwave before adding dried figs to it.) I also had a hot cross bun and black coffee made with the Aeropress.

DURING

On the bike I had a pre-prepped snack bag (stored in the top tube bag) that contained the following sweet and salty combo: Jelly Babies, salted peanuts, dried figs and soft liquorice. I had planned a handful every hour but that was tricky with hands in gloves! I also had three apple and pecan Raw Paleo bars.

I made two café stops and had a cheese scone, then a fruit scone.

I took two bidons – one with plain water, the other with an electrolyte dissolved in it. I had extra electrolyte tablets to add to bottles after refilling. Lunch in Alston sitting on the kerb in bright sunshine, I demolished a traditional audax lunch of an egg sandwich, an apple, a ginger and dark chocolate bar and a bag of cheese and onion crisps – all washed down with a can of Irn-Bru.

POST-RIDE

The 'arrivee' of the audax was a community centre where the organisers had minestrone soup, cheese rolls and Hobnobs on offer, plus several cups of tea – heaven.

ADVICE

- Fuelling can make or break a long day in the saddle. I try to take on 100–200 calories every hour and have learned to start eating after 1.5 hrs of riding, even if I don't feel hungry.

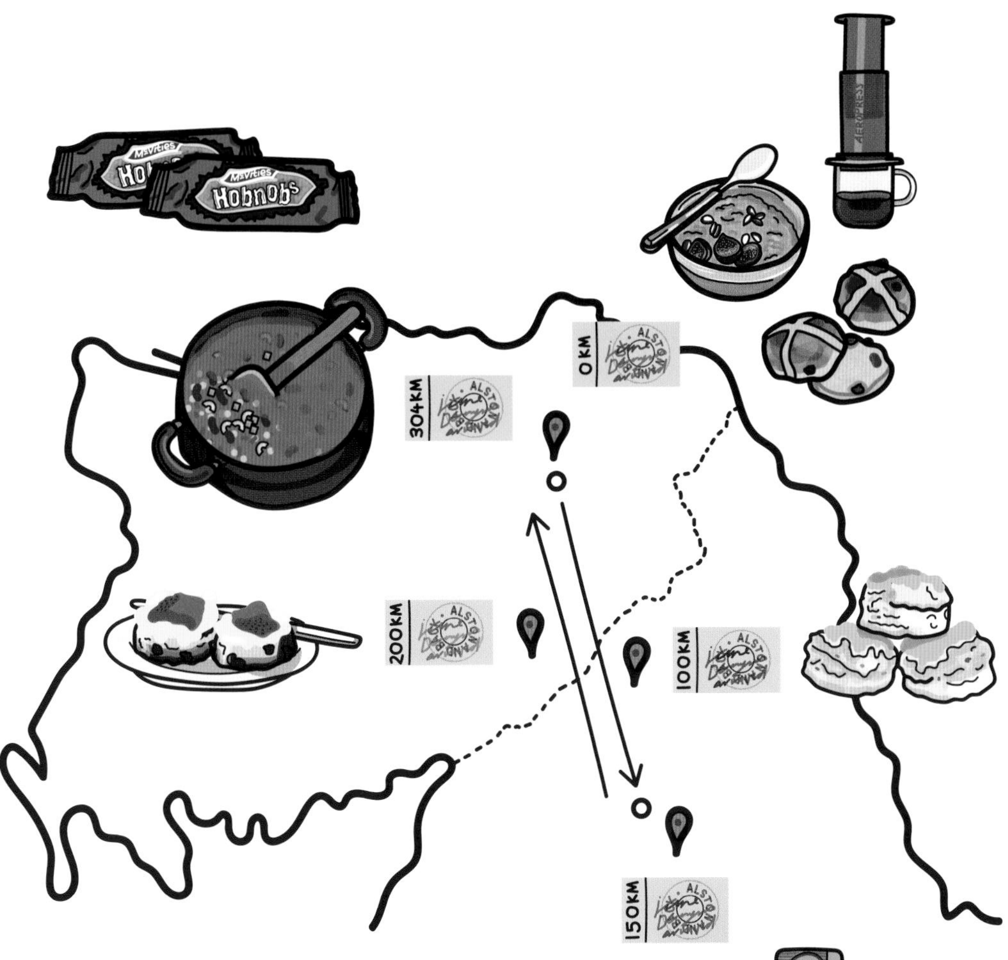

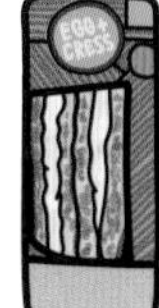

BAR BAG KEY:

1. Salted peanuts
2. Jelly Babies
3. Dried figs
4. Soft liquorice
5. Raw bars x 3

PATSY CRAIG

AGE 36
STIRLING, SCOTLAND

MOUNTAIN BIKER

Enjoys easy-going mountain biking and some magical mystery tours, which often end up in bogs!

THE RIDE

My weekly 1.5–2-hour adventure up local hills after work.

PRE-RIDE

I generally have something nice and stodgy at lunch time. Usually the go-to is nice and comforting homemade dahl; the secret ingredients are a glug of apple cider vinegar and soy sauce right at the end to give it a bit more depth, with a side of rice with some chopped coriander.

DURING

I always have a pocket snack of oatcakes, a tangerine and some homemade **energy balls** (dates, almond butter, coconut oil and cacao powder) just in case I feel the need to top up. I don't usually need them and they just get carried over into the next ride. Carrying the oatcakes in my pocket means they crumble to dust, which helpfully makes it easier to eat them from the bag (like a funnel of oaty, crunchy goodness) and no muddy hands touching the snacks!

POST-RIDE

When we come back and peel off our muddy kits, the urge to not do anything is strong, so we sometimes have **quesadillas**: two tortillas spread with homemade wild garlic pesto and a sprinkling of cheese, slapped together and heated in a frying pan.

ADVICE

- Don't forget to zip up your pockets. Snack loss is sad.

ENERGY BALLS, P.94; QUESADILLA, P.66

WORK
EAT
OUT
OF
OFFICE
HILLS
20%
RECOVER!

ENERGY BALLS

MAKES 12 BALLS

for the balls

250g pitted Medjool dates

180g almond or peanut butter

45g rolled oats

3 tbsp raw cacao powder

2 tbsp maca powder

for the toppings, if using (each covers 5–6 balls)

10g unsalted pistachios, finely ground in a pestle and mortar or food processor

10g freeze dried raspberries, crushed in a pestle and mortar or blitzed in a food processor

10g raw cacao powder

Wrap these like bonbons so they're ready to grab and go when you know you're going to need a bit of an energy grenade. Maca is a powdered root that is rich in iron, calcium, amino acids and vitamins and minerals, so it's bringing a lot to the party.

Put the dates, almond or peanut butter, oats, cacao and maca powders in a food processor and blitz until well incorporated. The mixture should come together quite quickly and form a ball. If not, add about 25ml water a splash at a time and blitz until the mixture is sticky but not pasty.

Now tip the mixture onto a surface with edges, such as a tray or large plate, and use clean hands to roll it into balls just smaller than ping pong balls. If rolling the balls in toppings, pour the topping of choice onto a tray or plate and roll the balls into it.

Store in an airtight container in the fridge for up to 2 weeks.

POST-

-RIDE

It's easy to forget the importance of replenishing your body's energy and fluid levels when your ride is over. You're super hungry, standing in front of the fridge and anything goes, right?

To get the full benefit from the food you eat post cycle, timing is key. As soon as you get off your bike, start replacing lost fluids and salts (hello, chocolate milk), but remember the window of opportunity between 20 minutes to an hour after your ride where your body can get the maximum benefit and fastest recovery from a protein-rich meal. This is when your muscles are particularly able to synthesise protein to do its job of building and repair. It doesn't need to be a huge meal, and, in fact, studies have shown that eating little and often can be beneficial post cycle. It helps to plan, as the last thing you will want to do is go to the shops or stand at the stove for half an hour. A quick omelette (p.100) is perfect, a pizza (p.129) ready to throw into the oven can be a wonder and a slow cooker ready and waiting with a warming restorative bean chilli (p.134) can be heaven.

POST-RIDE STAR FOODS

CHOCOLATE MILK

With its unique blend of casein and whey proteins, milk contains amino acids that are very similar in pattern to muscle protein and therefore make it very effective at repairing human muscle. Chocolate milk helps your body to replace muscle glycogen that is burned on an intense ride whilst also rehydrating you, and the sugar and sodium help you to retain water as you replenish your energy levels. It's a true après-sport recovery hero! However, choose brands that are low in processed sugar and don't contain baddies like corn syrup and palm oil.

BOOST YOUR PROTEIN INTAKE

Getting enough protein in your diet is important not just after a cycle but on a daily basis, as it gives you the nutritional building blocks to grow and restore muscle, build bone density and heal quickly. Obvious sources of protein are meat, fish and eggs but there are plant-based options too. Here are simple ways to introduce more protein into your meals and snacks.

For breakfast

- Add a swirl of nut butter to your porridge.
- Add pumpkin, sunflower or chia seeds to your granola.
- Swap in Greek yoghurt for your normal yoghurt.

For lunch

- Add a hardboiled egg to your packed lunch.
- Fill celery sticks with peanut butter as a great snack.
- Keep nuts handy to add to salads or to nibble on.
- Go big on lentils in soups or dahl.

For your evening meal

- Add beans to whatever you're having.
- Have protein-rich peas as a delicious side.
- Add tahini to salad dressings.
- Choose quinoa over rice and pasta.

KITTY'S OMURICE WITH CHEESE AND SPINACH

SERVES 1 TO 2

for the omelette

2 large eggs

2 tbsp finely chopped chives

¼ tsp sea salt

1 tbsp olive oil

50g meltable cheese such as Gruyère or Cheddar, grated

for the rice

1 tbsp olive oil

½ medium onion, finely chopped

100g cooked brown rice

12 spring onions, very finely chopped

100g baby spinach, larger stems removed

1 tbsp soy sauce

to serve

a handful of baby salad leaves

2 radishes, sliced

This is a perfect post-sport protein and carb lift as it can be prepared pretty instantly from basic ingredients. We've used spinach and spring onions here, but any greens will work. Traditionally, in Japan, a smiley face is drawn on the omelette in ketchup, which I heartily recommend as a delicious serving suggestion.

First, beat the eggs well in a medium bowl, then add the chives and salt and mix. Set aside.

Now for the rice. Heat the olive oil in a saucepan, add the onion and cook on a medium heat until translucent, about 2–3 minutes. Stir in the cooked rice, spring onions and spinach, then turn the heat to low, put the lid on and let the spinach steam for 5 minutes. Stir well, add the soy sauce, then take off the heat and set aside.

Whilst the rice is still hot, heat the tablespoon of olive oil in a heavy-based frying pan. Let it get medium hot (you want the egg mixture to sizzle as it hits the oil), then give the mixture a stir and add it to the pan, swirling it so it covers the base evenly. Scatter the cheese evenly over the egg mixture.

Working quickly, arrange the hot rice mixture in a neat even line across the middle of the omelette. Using a spatula, gently bring the bottom part of the omelette up over the top of the rice, then roll the omelette away from you so the top third is on the bottom and the omelette is sealed. Finally, slide it off the edge of the pan and onto your plate and eat immediately.

Serve with some salad leaves and sliced radishes.

PREP 10–30MIN
MAKE 10MIN

BUILDABLE SALADS

SERVES 1

Three Easy Delicious Dressings:

Honey Mustard

2 tsp wholegrain mustard

2 tsp honey

juice of 1 lemon

6 tbsp extra virgin olive oil

sea salt and freshly ground pepper

Herby Dressing

15g basil leaves, chopped

1 teaspoon Dijon mustard

1 tbsp white wine vinegar

½ clove garlic, grated

3 tbsp extra virgin olive oil

Mint Dressing

15g mint leaves, chopped

75g cucumber, deseeded and grated

125g Greek yoghurt

1 tbsp sherry vinegar

zest of 1 lemon

sea salt and freshly ground pepper

For salad to work as a post-cycle evening meal, it's got to be hearty and delicious enough to fill the gap. Choose one or more ingredients from the following categories below and drizzle with a dressing (see left).

1. One handful each **Greens**: lettuce, kale, spinach, pea shoots, watercress, rocket or beetroot tops; **Raw Vegetables**: grated beetroot, red cabbage, mushrooms, carrots or peppers; **Cooked Vegetables**: grilled sweetcorn cut off the cob, roasted peppers or steamed courgette; **Fruit**: sliced apple, mango or nectarine.

2. One palm-size portion **Protein**: grilled or roast chicken, steamed or seared salmon, grilled prawns, seared scallops, seared steak; cheese: feta or seared halloumi; tofu, tempeh or seitan.

3. Two handfuls **Carbohydrates and Fibre**: roasted potatoes, black-eyed beans, cannellini beans, chick-peas, Puy lentils, quinoa, brown rice or wholegrain pasta.

4. One tbsp **Seeds and Nuts**: hazelnuts, macadamia nuts, smoked almonds or salted cashews; sunflower, sesame or chia seeds, chickpeas or pumpkin seeds roasted quickly in tamari; pomegranate seeds.

5. One handful chopped **Fresh Herbs**: basil, coriander, tarragon or mint; 1 tbsp **Spices**: chilli flakes or toasted coriander seeds; toasted nori sheets cut into strips; hot sauce.

6. Two tbsp **Dressing** (see left, also Miso Dressing, p.125; Tahini Dressing, p.79).

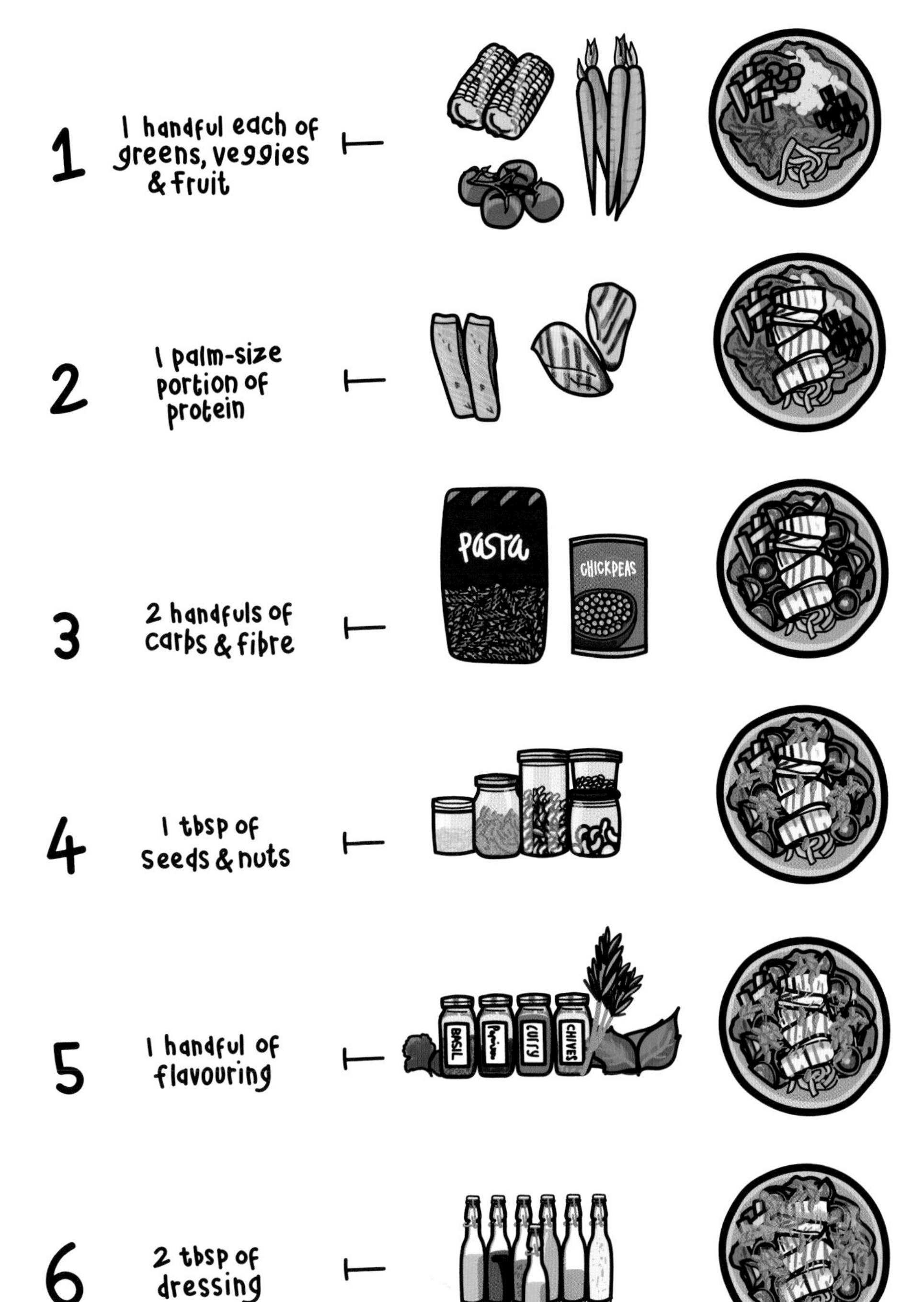
1
1 handful each of greens, veggies & fruit
2
1 palm-size portion of protein
PASTA
CHICKPEAS
3
2 handfuls of carbs & fibre
4
1 tbsp of seeds & nuts
BASIL
CURRY
CHIVES
5
1 handful of flavouring
6
2 tbsp of dressing

CHICKPEA CURRY WITH COCONUT CHUTNEY

SERVES 4

1 tbsp sunflower oil

1 large onion, finely chopped

1 tsp ground turmeric

25g fresh ginger, grated

2 medium green serrano chillies, deseeded and finely chopped

2 garlic cloves, finely chopped

1 x 400g tin chickpeas, drained and rinsed

1 tbsp garam masala or tikka masala curry paste

1 x 400g tin plum tomatoes, chopped

small handful of coriander, finely chopped

salt

for the coconut chutney

75g desiccated coconut

30g fresh coriander

1 tsp coriander seeds

zest and juice of 1 lime

¼ teaspoon fine sea salt

This version of chana masala is super simple and delicious, and because it's protein-rich and full of complex carbohydrates, it's a perfect post-cycle meal.

In a large heavy-based saucepan, heat the oil and add the onion, stirring occasionally until it softens, about 2–3 minutes. Then add the turmeric, ginger, chillies and garlic, and stir so that everything is covered in the oil and starts to cook.

Now add the chickpeas to the mixture, stirring well to incorporate. Cook for 2–3 minutes, then stir in the garam masala or tikka masala paste, the tomatoes and 200ml water and bring everything to a simmer. Cook for 30 minuntes until the sauce has thickened a little. Stir in the coriander and taste for seasoning. While the chickpeas are simmering, make the chutney. Put the coconut, coriander, coriander seeds, lime zest and juice, salt and a tablespoon of water in a food processor and blitz until blended. Transfer to a bowl.

Serve with flatbread or pitta, generous spoonfuls of the chutney and a wedge of lime.

Easy flatbreads

Measure 350g Greek yoghurt (not fat-free), 350g self-raising flour and ½ tsp salt. In a bowl, mix 300g flour with the salt and yoghurt. Mix to a dough and divide into four pieces, then use the remaining 50g flour to dust a board. Roll each piece of dough into a circle about 5mm thick and cook in a heavy-based frying pan over medium heat until browned, about 2–3 minutes on each side.

TIFFANY CROMWELL

AGE 32
MONACO

PROFESSIONAL ROAD RACER

Loves off-road disciplines like mountain biking and gravel biking as well as road racing.

THE RIDE

World Championships Road Race, 150km, Harrogate, UK.

PRE-RIDE

Porridge with nut butter and maple syrup, topped with Greek yoghurt, bananas and berries. When possible I have a flat white; otherwise I make an Aeropress coffee.

Worlds is normally raced at around 1pm, and I generally begin carb loading 3 hours before the race. I had a bowl of **pasta with tomato sauce** and some Parmesan cheese.

DURING

I usually opt for gels as they're the easiest to consume when racing. For a 4-hour predicted race, I take enough food to have something every 30 minutes, plus an Emergency Extra. Six SiS gels, one SiS caffeine gel for the business end of the race and one to two rice cakes for a little bit of real food. I start with two bidons, one with SiS Beta-Fuel and one with water or a hydro tab.

POST-RIDE

Worlds is normally the last race of the season, so this is where we get stuck into all the good things we've been trying to avoid when in top shape. I will sometimes have a recovery shake but after this race I had an Indian, a G&T and cake.

ADVICE

- Refuel regularly and start early – if you wait until you're hungry, you're usually too late and you will probably pay for it when it counts.
- If you know your race hotel isn't going to have good coffee, always pack your own. I take fresh beans, a grinder and an Aeropress or V60. It makes all the difference if you can avoid having to consume bad coffee.

POWER OATS, P.32; MAGIC ONE-POT PASTA, P.108

RACE
FUEL
START
FINISH
GEL
GEL
GEL
EL
EL
Tiff's Rice cake
END OF
SEASON
cheers

MAGIC ONE-POT PASTA

SERVES 2

4 tbsp olive oil

1 onion, finely chopped

2 garlic cloves, finely chopped

250g dry pasta, preferably penne or rigatoni

½ glass white wine

200g roasted peppers (from a jar is fine), chopped

8–10 sun-blushed tomatoes, chopped

1 x 400g tin chopped tomatoes

400ml vegetarian stock (made with a jelly stock cube)

1 tsp brown sugar

1 tsp red wine vinegar

½ tsp sea salt

handful of basil leaves, chopped

50g Parmesan cheese, freshly grated

To tell you the truth, the magic in this pasta is that it's just really tasty and easy to cook. There's no trick to it; you're essentially just cooking the pasta like risotto rice.

Heat the olive oil in a large, wide pan and add the onion and garlic. Fry for 2–3 minutes, or until the onion is fragrant and translucent, then add the pasta and stir well to coat it in the oniony oil. This should take about 2 minutes.

Turn up the heat a little and add the white wine. You should hear it sizzle. Give everything a stir, then add the roasted peppers and sun-blushed tomatoes.

Now add the chopped tomatoes, stock, brown sugar, red wine vinegar and salt and stir again.

Leave to simmer, uncovered, for 15 minutes, stirring occasionally, making sure the pasta is mostly under the sauce cooking. It is done when the pasta is cooked but still firm and the sauce has come together.

Serve with a sprinkling of the basil and some grated Parmesan cheese.

DOVILE BASKAKOVAITE

AGE 29
SWITZERLAND

ROAD RIDER

Likes quick post-work rides to clear the head and weekend long rides (preferably uphill).

THE RIDE

A typical 3–4-hour 80km weekend ride + 1000m elevation gain.

PRE-RIDE

I was looking for new recipe ideas online and came across this **oven-baked oat porridge** which which makes a perfect pre-workout meal. You can add whatever you like to it, as with regular porridge (coconut oil, coconut flakes and cacao nibs are my faves), but baking makes it so much tastier – more like a cake!

DURING

High-carb snacks – ridiculously cheap soft fruit bars from Aldi or Lidl instead of energy bars for cycling. Caramel waffles (or stroopwafels) which I pack into my jersey back pocket so they get warm and melty and all-round delicious.

POST-RIDE

Carbonara with double cream, please (because I love it!).

ADVICE

- Pack a boiled egg in your jersey pocket. If you need to fuel quickly after a ride and there's nowhere nearby to eat, it might do the trick (an ultimate saviour from the (h)angriness).
- Planning ahead always helps, unless you're riding in Italy or France where you're in gelateria and patisserie heaven – then go get that gelato or pain au chocolat!

CHERRY, CHOCOLATE AND COCONUT BAKED OATS, P.51; CARBONARA, P.113

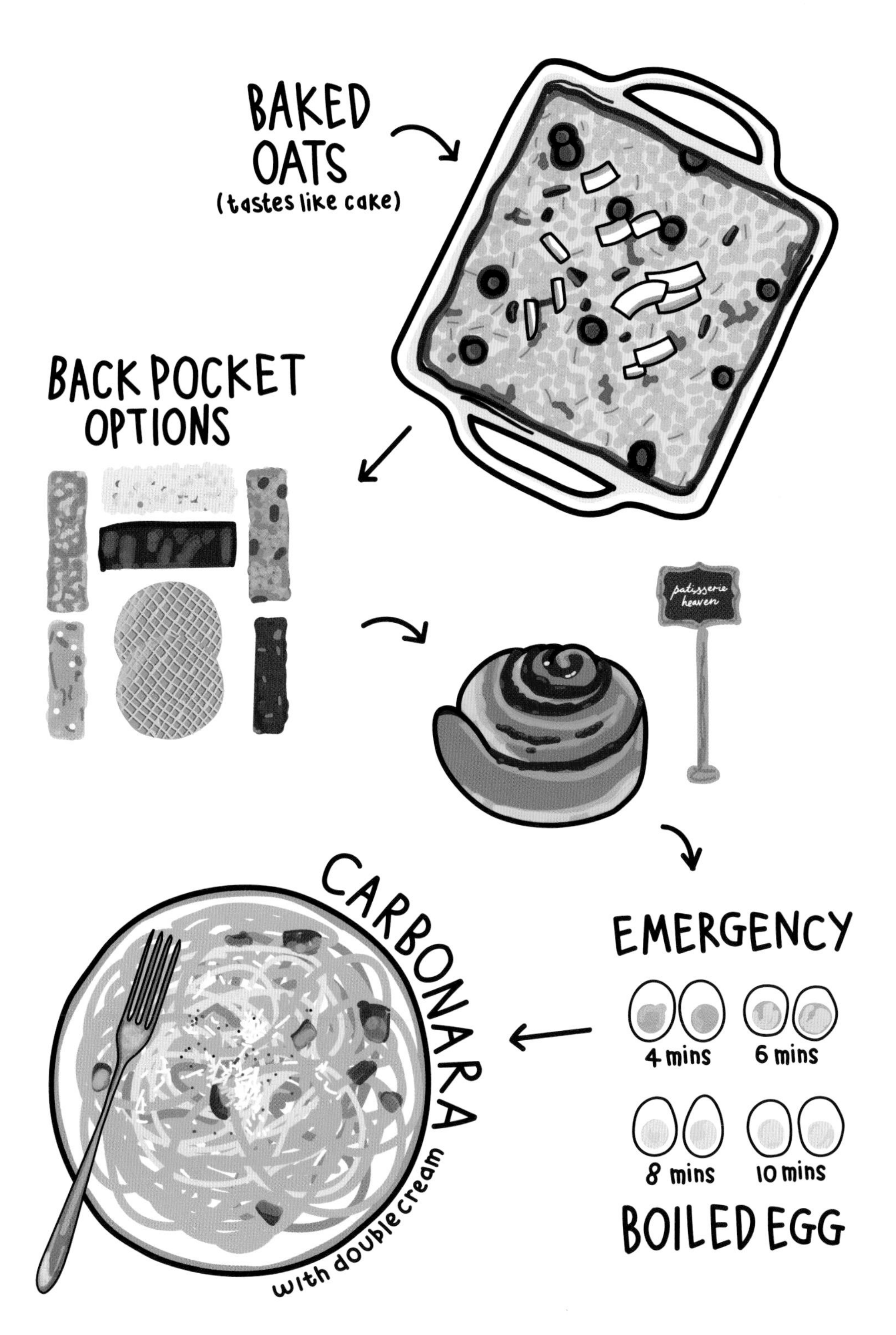
BAKED OATS
(tastes like cake)
BACK POCKET OPTIONS
patisserie heaven
EMERGENCY
4 mins
6 mins
8 mins
10 mins
BOILED EGG
CARBONARA
with double cream

CARBONARA

SERVES 2

150g pancetta or smoked streaky bacon, chopped into chunky strips

salt

200g dry spaghetti

2 large eggs plus 1 yolk

40g Parmesan or Pecorino Romano cheese, freshly grated, plus extra to serve

50ml double cream (optional)

freshly ground black pepper

small handful of parsley, chopped (optional)

There is no cream in a classic carbonara but its addition is merited by any cycling cook looking to add ultra-richness to this delicious comfort food.

Place a large frying pan over a medium heat and add the pancetta or bacon. As it slowly cooks, the fat will render and give you the first part of the carbonara sauce.

Put a large pan of salted water on to boil and cook the spaghetti to al dente according to the instructions on the packet.

While the spaghetti is cooking, break the eggs into a large bowl, add the yolk, the grated cheese and the double cream, if using, and whisk together with generous quantities of black pepper. Set aside.

Magically, everything should be ready at the same time. When the pancetta or bacon is brown and the fat has rendered, the pasta should be ready. Turn off the heat under the bacon pan.

Turn off the heat under the pasta and tong it out of the cooking water into the pan with the browned pancetta or bacon (you want the residual water to cool the pan down a bit). Use the tongs to mix the pasta with the bacon. There should be no sizzling now.

Now add the egg and cheese mixture and stir it gently into the pasta, ensuring the long strands are coated with the sauce. Finally, season with more black pepper, sprinkle with the parsley, if using, and serve immediately.

PREP 5MIN

COOK 30MIN

MUSHROOM RISOTTO

SERVES 2

6 tbsp olive oil

250g shallots, finely chopped

1 garlic clove, finely chopped

250g Arborio rice

250ml dry white wine

900ml vegetarian stock

50g butter

200g mushrooms (such as chestnut, shitake or chanterelle), sliced

sea salt

1 tbsp fresh lemon juice

a handful of flat leaf parsley, roughly chopped

salt and freshly ground black pepper

50g Parmesan, freshly grated (optional)

Risotto is comfort food, ideal for post-ride recovery, and very easy to conjure out of a storecupboard with very little in it. Here is a hearty, warming mushroom version but you could substitute other vegetables too, as in the spring variation inspired by Victoria Gill's green risotto (see variation, right).

Add the olive oil to a heavy-based sauté pan and warm over a medium heat. Add the shallots and garlic and cook until the shallots are soft and beginning to turn golden. Add the rice and stir around in the pan so that each grain is coated with the shallot-scented oil.

Turn up the heat slightly and add the white wine to the pan. Let it come to quite a vigorous simmer, stirring from time to time, and cook until the wine has almost disappeared. Then, turning down the heat a wee bit, add a third of the stock and keep stirring until it's almost completely absorbed. Add the rest of the stock 300ml at a time until it's all been absorbed and the rice is becoming tender and creamy. (This should take about 20 minutes.)

While the risotto is simmering, cook your mushrooms. Add half of the butter to a large frying pan on a medium heat and sauté until they are softened and brown, about 5–7 minutes. Finish with a pinch of salt and the lemon juice, then set aside.

After about 20 minutes, test a grain or two of rice – it should be tender with no hint of hardness, and not mushy. Quickly stir the rest of the butter into the risotto, then fold in the mushrooms and the parsley. Taste and season to your liking. Serve straight away, topped with the grated Parmesan, if using.

VARIATION

Spring risotto

Omit the mushrooms and instead fry 100g baby asparagus in olive oil seasoned with ½ tsp salt and a squeeze of lemon juice and add to the risotto along with 75g frozen or fresh petit pois and 75g washed, stemmed baby spinach when you would have added the mushrooms. Substitute mint for the parsley and crème fraîche for the Parmesan.

TIP

It is possible to cook risotto in advance: simply take the pan off the heat after the second addition of stock and pour the risotto into a wide, flat baking dish (so it cools quickly), and refrigerate for up to 2 days. When you're ready to finish the risotto, heat the remaining stock, put the risotto back into the heavy-based pan, add the hot stock and cook over a low heat, stirring occasionally, until the stock is absorbed and the risotto comes to a slow, steady simmer. Prepare your mushrooms and cook from this point as above.

STEAK WITH CHIMICHURRI AND ROASTED SWEET POTATOES

SERVES 2

for the sweet potatoes

3 sweet potatoes, peeled and cut into 3cm cubes

3 tbsp olive oil

1 tablespoon paprika or smoked paprika

½ tsp sea salt

1 tsp freshly ground black pepper

1 large onion, peeled and cut into chunky wedges or cubes

for the chimichurri

large handful of flat leaf parsley, chopped

small handful of coriander, chopped

a few sprigs of oregano

2 cloves garlic, peeled

juice of 2 limes

½ tsp red chilli flakes

½ tsp sea salt flakes

30ml red wine vinegar

120ml extra virgin olive oil

This recipe was inspired by Alison Jackson's bison steak dinner. In case you don't have access to bison, we've used a classic rib eye here, although, truly, it would be delicious made with seared cauliflower steak, chicken breasts or grilled sea bass. Any leftover chimichurri will keep in the fridge and is excellent with Slow-cooker Spicy Bean Chili (p.134).

Preheat the oven to 180°C/160°C fan.

In a large bowl, toss the sweet potatoes in the olive oil, then add the paprika and seasoning and toss again. Transfer everything in the bowl to a baking sheet, cover with foil, then pop in the oven for 20 minutes. Put the onion into the bowl you used to season the potatoes and give it a good swirl in the remaining spicy oil. After 20 minutes, take the foil off the roasting sweet potatoes and add the onion, giving everything a good mix to ensure it is covered in the hot roasting oil, then put them back in the oven for another 15–20 minutes.

Meanwhile make the chimichurri. Put the parsley, coriander, oregano, garlic, lime juice, chilli flakes, salt and vinegar in a food processor and whizz, or use a mixing wand. Once mixed, transfer to a bowl and slowly whisk in the olive oil.

for the steak

2 x 200g rib eye or rump steaks

1 tbsp olive oil

salt and freshly ground black pepper

Finally, sear the steaks. Heat a grill pan over high heat. Rub the steaks with the olive oil and season very generously. Grill until medium rare, about 2–4 minutes per side, depending on thickness. (The centre of the steak should register 52°C (125°F) on an instant-read thermometer.) Remove to a plate and allow to rest for at least 5 minutes before serving with the sweet potatoes and a few spoonfuls of the chimichurri.

SARAH CLARK

Likes weekend rides, riding holidays (on road or gravel) and mountain biking.

AGE 42
LONDON AND KENT, UK

ROAD RIDER AND EX-RACER

THE RIDE

Asia 5-day stage race, 120km per day.

PRE-RIDE

Two days before: for maximum hydration: 3 litres of water and electrolytes, regularly sipped throughout the day. This is even more important than carb loading!

During race week: avoid too much booze but one small glass of red wine won't hurt, especially if you are a regular drinker. (A glass while chatting to teammates helped me to relax and stopped me going to bed fixated on the next day.)

Breakfast on race day: cereal with fresh or dried fruit; two hard boiled eggs, two slices ham, two slices brown toast; tea – enough for caffeine but not so much that you need to pee mid-race... a very careful balance!

DURING

On the bike: SiS GO energy bars, fistfuls of Haribo, tiny bananas (easier to eat and really enough to give calories without discomfort); for constant hydration: SiS GO energy drink in one bottle; SiS electrolytes with caffeine in another.

POST-RIDE

Immediately after: I had a SiS REGO chocolate milk recovery drink and salty crackers.

Dinner: have a balanced plate that includes some carbs, some meat to give your stomach something to work on (runny tummy needs to be avoided, especially when your stomach isn't getting a proper meal during the day), and some veg to keep up your vitamins and minerals. Treat yourself to your favourite dessert; race week isn't a time to lose weight.

ADVICE

- Never try something new on race day. Stick to tried and tested foods. Practise your nutrition on training rides to find out what works for you.
- Hydration starts 2 days before multi-stage riding, especially in hot climates. You need to go into the week hydrated and stay hydrated. If you suffer from cramps, consider taking daily salt tablets.

2 DAYS BEFORE

HOTEL BREAKFAST

RACE FOOD

(eat + drink every hour)

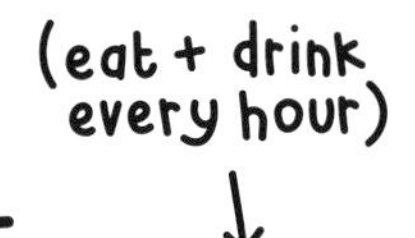

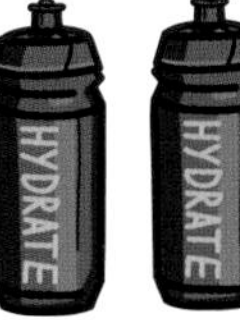

FINISH LINE

EVENING MEAL

RELAX

PREP 20MIN
COOK 15MIN

RAINBOW MISO BOWL

SERVES 2

2 large eggs, at room temperature

100g soba noodles

100g kale, tough stems removed, finely sliced

1 red pepper, finely sliced

150g red cabbage, finely sliced

1 courgette, sliced into fine ribbons with a peeler

1 ripe avocado, halved and finely sliced

1 spring onion, finely sliced on the diagonal

sea salt and freshly ground black pepper

1 tbsp sesame seeds

for the miso dressing

2 tbsp white miso

2 tbsp tahini

1 garlic clove, grated

20g fresh ginger, grated

20ml soy or tamari

20ml rice vinegar

20ml maple syrup

20ml sesame oil

Whatever you don't have for this recipe can be replaced with whatever you do have. Have fun; keep it delicious.

First bring a pan of salted water to the boil and cook the eggs for exactly 6½ minutes. Set a bowl of ice-cold water close by. When the eggs are done, remove them from the water and immerse them immediately in the cold water. This will give you perfectly cooked eggs with orange 'jammy' yolks.

To cook the soba noodles, bring another pan of water to the boil (but do not add salt). Add the noodles and simmer for 5–8 minutes, or according to the packet instructions. When the noodles are ready, drain them in a colander and rinse under cold water to remove excess starch and prevent them sticking together.

To make the miso dressing, in a large bowl, dissolve the miso and the tahini in 30–45ml hot water, then whisk in the remaining ingredients.

Toss the noodles in 2–3 tablespoons of the dressing, then divide between your serving bowls. Peel and halve the eggs. Arrange the vegetables and then the eggs on top of the noodles. Finally, drizzle with the miso dressing, season and scatter over the sesame seeds.

SUSAN ROBERTS

AGE 46
MANCHESTER, UK

ROAD RIDER

Loves riding with friends; enjoys endurance long-distance rides, sportives, time trials and track.

THE RIDE

Manchester to London Rapha Ride (354km, 14 hours).

PRE-RIDE

Two porridge pots (the ones with lots of fruit and sugar!) before we started, then lots of croissants.

DURING

Every 20 minutes I have cheesy cheddar snacks and crêpes filled with chocolate – I buy the pre-wrapped ones that you get from the supermarket. I cut the tops off the packets so I can eat them like ice pops and keep them in my bar bag. I also eat Clif shot blocks, which are just like Jelly Babies but probably more expensive.

My emergency supplies are Squashies (lovely pink and white goodness that will get you out of a dark place).

At food stops, I opt for sandwiches and cheesy chips, especially around tea time.

My secret sauce drink is diluted, full fat Coke – 50% water and 50% Coke.

POST-RIDE

Pizza and a bottle of beer! (Not what sports nutritionists want to hear!)

ADVICE

- My favourite back pocket snack is cheese and pickle sandwiches. They always make you feel better – and stronger! If there's an opportunity, I do love an iced bun.

MANCHESTER
HONEY + A
Oats
HONEY + A
Oats
CLIF SHOT BLOKS
CLIF SHOT BLOKS
REPEAT
MINI
ORIGINAL
EMERGENCY SUPPLIES
SOS
squashies
Coca-Cola
PIT STOP
CHEESE PLEASE
ALE
ALE
LONDON

PREP 75MIN + 2H
BAKE 15MIN

PIZZA

MAKES 8 X 10–12" PIZZAS, DEPENDING HOW THICK YOU LIKE THEM

for the sauce

1 tbsp extra virgin olive oil

2 garlic cloves, finely chopped

2 x 400g tins chopped tomatoes

2 tbsp tomato purée

1 tbsp dried oregano

1 tbsp brown sugar

1 tbsp red wine vinegar

for the pizza

2 x 7g sachets fast action dried yeast

1 tbsp honey or agave syrup

1kg Italian 00 flour, preferably, but plain white flour will do (the dough will just be a little less light)

100ml extra virgin olive oil

1 tsp sea salt

4 tbsp coarse polenta

500g mozzarella cheese (approx. 1 x 125g ball per 2 pizzas), thinly sliced

This quantity of dough will make eight medium pizzas. If you don't want to make a batch to freeze, you can halve the recipe and it will work perfectly. If you want to be very organised, freeze the sauce into pizza-sized portions and store with the dough. This is the basic pizza and sauce recipe. It's up to you to be as creative as you like with the toppings.

To make the sauce, put the olive oil, garlic, tomatoes, tomato purée, oregano, sugar and vinegar in a medium pan and simmer for an hour, then set aside until needed. This recipe makes enough sauce for eight pizzas so if you are making it to freeze, do so now in pizza-sized portions.

To make the pizza dough, in a jug dissolve the yeast and honey or agave syrup in 600ml warm water, then set aside for 5 minutes while the yeast blossoms and activates.

Sift the flour into a large bowl and make a hollow in the center of the pile. Pour the olive oil and salt into the hollow and cover it over with flour.

Once the yeast has developed a Guinness-like head and has started to generate some bubbles, add it into the flour. Now incorporate everything and start mixing. You can do this with the dough hooks on a hand blender, a stand mixer or by hand.

Quite quickly you will see the dough coming together; stop when it starts to look smooth and stretchy and all the stray bits of flour from the sides of the bowl have been absorbed. Form it into a large ball. When you poke this with your finger the dimple made should gently spring back. Cover with a clean, damp tea towel and set aside for 1–2 hours, until it has doubled in size.

When you're ready to make your pizza, preheat the oven to 240°C/220°C fan – or the hottest it will go.

Tip everything out onto a large, clean, floured surface and sprinkle a bit of flour over the dough. Pat into a large square and with a sharp knife divide it into 8 equal pieces. Set aside the pieces you don't need (knead) today and roll them into balls ready for freezing. Rub the surface of the balls with olive oil in your hands and put them into individual zipper bags, squeezing the air out as you seal them. Write the date on the bags and freeze.

When you're ready to bake the pizza, prep your baking trays by sprinkling a tablespoon of polenta over the surface – this will stop the dough sticking and help the base become firm instead of soggy. Roll or stretch out the dough into a rough circle, transfer onto the baking tray and top with the sauce, a few slices of mozzarella cheese and anything else you fancy. The thinner the dough has been rolled, the shorter the cooking time will be so you will need to use your judgement, but check after 8–10 minutes. If the cheese is brown and bubbly, that's the sign you're looking for.

TIP

A ball of frozen pizza dough should defrost nicely in a couple of hours. Simply take it out of the freezer bag, place in a bowl, rub the top with olive oil again and cover with a damp tea towel. Leave in a warm place, cycle like the very wind and it will be waiting for you on your return. Turn on the oven to heat up before you go for your shower.

TOULOUSE SAUSAGE AND PUY LENTIL CASSEROLE

SERVES 4

2 tbsp olive oil

8 Toulouse sausages, or any other good-quality (min. 75% meat) sausage such as Italian style with fennel, chilli and garlic

1 large onion, finely chopped

1 stick celery, finely chopped

2 medium carrots, peeled and finely chopped

3 garlic cloves, finely chopped

100ml red wine

250g Puy lentils, rinsed under cold water in a sieve

500ml chicken stock

large sprig of fresh rosemary

large sprig of fresh thyme

salt and freshly ground black pepper

This is the kind of rich warming food that only needs a big green salad dressed with sharp mustardy dressing to go with it. As well as body repair, it is soul repair.

Heat 1 tablespoon of olive oil in the casserole over a medium heat, add the sausages and brown all over – this should take about 10 minutes. When they're golden, transfer the sausages to a plate, add the second tablespoon of the olive oil to the casserole and sauté the onion, celery and carrots for 5–6 minutes, until they start to soften and become fragrant. Then add the garlic and continue to sauté for a further 2 minutes.

Turn the heat under the casserole up a little, let the vegetables start to brown and catch a bit, then add the red wine. Use a wooden spoon to scrape any slightly burnt bits of sausage and onion that have stuck to the bottom of the pan – you are mining flavour gold here. Let the wine reduce a bit and start to concentrate for a couple of minutes.

Then return the sausages to the casserole, pour in the rinsed Puy lentils, the stock, the rosemary and the thyme (reserving a few leaves to sprinkle over when serving) and bring everything to a gentle simmer over a low heat.

Put the lid on the casserole and allow to simmer for 45 minutes, stirring from time to time to make sure it's not sticking on the bottom. After 45 minutes, everything should be tender. Season to taste, chop the reserved rosemary and thyme and sprinkle over the hot casserole before serving.

SLOW-COOKER SPICY BEAN CHILLI

SERVES 4, GENEROUSLY

- 25ml olive oil
- ½ red onion, finely chopped
- 2 sticks celery, finely chopped
- 1 red pepper, finely diced
- 1 yellow pepper, finely diced
- 10–15 sundried tomatoes in oil, finely chopped
- 2 garlic cloves, finely chopped
- 1 tsp paprika
- ½ tsp ground cinnamon
- 1 tsp ground coriander
- 2 tsp your favourite hot sauce
- 2 x 400g tins beans such as black beans, cannellini beans, haricot, butter beans or chickpeas
- 1 x 400g tin of really good-quality chopped tomatoes
- 1 vegetable stock cube
- approx. 400ml of fruity red wine, or water if you prefer
- salt and freshly ground black pepper

This hearty, flavoursome chilli is wonderful served as it is but is also easily customised at the table with Quick Pickled Red Onion (see box, right), Pico de Gallo (p.64) or Chimichurri (p.118). Leftover chilli freezes well and is delicious in a burrito or as a filling for a baked sweet potato.

In a large frying pan, heat the olive oil and add the onion, celery, peppers, sundried tomatoes and garlic. Sauté for 5 minutes, stirring occasionally, until everything starts to soften. Now stir in the paprika, cinnamon, ground coriander and the hot sauce and continue to cook for another 5 minutes.

Turn the slow cooker to hot and transfer the spicy vegetable mix into it. Add the beans, tomatoes and stock cube, and mix well, ensuring everything is submerged in liquid. If it isn't, add red wine or water until it is.

Turn the heat down and simmer on medium for 4 hours, by which time the sauce will have thickened and become rich. Check for seasoning and adjust to your taste.

Serve in a big bowl with some or all of the sides and customise to your liking.

to serve

crème fraîche

handful of coriander, roughly chopped

6 spring onions, finely sliced, or Quick Pickled Red Onion (see box)

tacos or tortilla chips

grated Cheddar

QUICK PICKLED RED ONION

½ red onion, finely sliced

2 bay leaves

100ml white wine vinegar

1 tbsp soft brown sugar

1 tbsp mustard seeds

1 tbsp coriander seeds

Put the onion and bay leaves in a bowl or clean jar just big enough to hold them.

In a small pan, heat the vinegar, sugar and spices to a simmer, then pour over the onion.

Leave for 10 minutes and eat, or store in the fridge for up to 2 weeks.

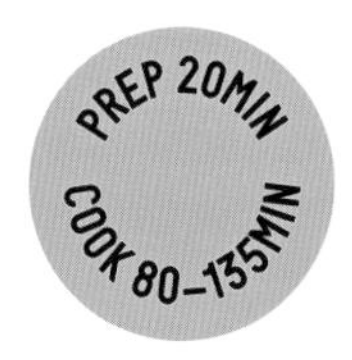

CLASSIC BEEF CASSEROLE

SERVES 4

1kg beef shin, cut into even 3cm cubes

100g plain flour, well-seasoned with sea salt and freshly ground black pepper

50ml olive oil

1 onion, chopped

2 carrots, peeled and sliced into lengths

1 tbsp tomato purée

1 garlic clove, finely chopped

200ml fruity red wine such as Merlot

300ml beef stock

a bouquet garni (2 sprigs thyme, 2 sprigs rosemary, 2–3 parsley stems and a fresh bay leaf wrapped in the hollow of two sticks of celery or the green of a leek and tied up with string)

to serve

zest of 1 orange

a sprig of rosemary, leaves only, very finely chopped

This hearty stew is just as good – some would argue better – served the day after it's made. If you are finishing this in the oven, make baked potatoes at the same time.

In a bowl, toss the beef in the seasoned flour. Then in a decently sized casserole, heat half the olive oil over a medium heat and fry the beef in batches (3 should do it) until it is well browned. As each batch browns, transfer it to a bowl on the side. Frying the beef in stages ensures it browns – if the batches are too big, the casserole can't get hot enough and the meat starts to boil in its own juice. Once all the beef has been seared, add the remaining olive oil to the casserole and fry the onion for 8–10 minutes, until softened. Then add the carrots, tomato purée and garlic. Stir often, scraping any vegetables that catch on the bottom of the pan, until they are golden.

Now add the red wine to the hot casserole (it should cause noisy bubbling). Turn down the heat and, using a wooden spoon, scrape all the caramelised bits of beef and vegetables until they dissolve into the wine. The sauce will start to thicken almost straight away.

Add the beef, its juices, the stock and the bouquet garni and stir once. Put the lid on the casserole, turn the heat down to low and simmer gently for 1½ hours, or until the meat is so tender you can cut it with a spoon. If you prefer, put the casserole in a preheated oven (160°C/140°C fan) for 2½–3 hours, checking it and giving it a stir every hour. Combine the orange zest and rosemary in a small bowl. Serve the stew with a small pinch of the orange-rosemary seasoning to add a zing.

REBECCA CHARLTON

BRIGHTON, UK

ROAD AND TRACK RIDER

Loves track racing; her favourite discipline to watch, race and report on is the Madison. Sipping tea at Herne Hill velodrome on a Saturday morning with friends is bliss.

THE RIDE

Rapha Women's 100 (a 100km ride).

PRE-RIDE

Breakfast like a queen! **Porridge** every time, with raw brown sugar and a banana. Then a skimmed milk latte and orange juice.

DURING

The key is quick-release, morale-boosting food that won't melt in the pocket: sweets, muesli bars and a veggie sandwich. If there's a shop, I'll buy crisps to put in the sandwich and JAFFA CAKES! If I'm really hanging, I have a gel. Coffee and tea wherever possible.

POST-RIDE

PROSECCO and carbs! Probably a veggie burger and chips (I am in no way endorsing the nutritional value of this choice!).

POWER OATS, P.32

BREAKFAST

NO MELTING HERE
SUGAR
CAFE STOP
always
COFFEE & TEA
WALKERS
EXTRA SALT
RIDE FUEL
VEG
"PROSECCO & CARBS"

INDEX

ACKNOWLEDGEMENTS

KITTY PEMBERTON-PLATT

For the creative encouragement, for giving me purpose and for the ongoing inspiration – thank you:

My family.

My lifelong friends - 'LCQs', Scarpa Racing, 'Godivas' and all the other women I've met on the bike.

The Midnight Club.

Kitchen Press.

And, my Joe. X

FI BUCHANAN

Fondest thanks to Lucas, who is my light.

Grateful thanks to Nasim for her friendship and guidance.